Sharing My Faith

A Teen's Guide to Evangelism

Edited by
Mark Gilroy

Beacon Hill Press of Kansas City
Kansas City, Missouri

10   9   8   7   6   5   4   3   2   1

Contents

Introduction
The Edge of the Ledge

I was 17 years old, driving through the Smoky Mountains on family vacation. My family hit that saturation point where at the same time everyone feels an intense claustrophobia and has to be out of the car. Just off the road ahead there was a clearing beside a cool Tennessee stream with about 10 cars parked there—we must not have been the only ones that got claustrophobia. Just about 10 yards further down, the stream turned into a pool. Thirty-three feet above the pool was a ledge that was perfectly situated for diving.

I decided I had to dive the 33 feet into the pool. Maybe I was feeling the need to prove my manhood. That's a major issue at age 17. I confidently strode up the path that led to the ledge. And I confidently walked to the edge. Then I looked down. I suddenly didn't want to jump anymore. The problem is that about 25 people, including my family, and especially my two sisters, had already seen my intention. To back down now would be to lose face—no way to prove your manhood. Well, it wasn't a pretty sight. But after about five minutes of mustering my courage, with my heart pounding, I dove.

The fact that you are holding this book in your hands might mean you, too, are on the edge of the ledge. Maybe you've come to a point in your life where you feel it is time to start witnessing to friends. Maybe a youth leader or pastor or parent is exerting some pressure for you to start sharing your faith. Whatever the case, my guess is that when you think about actually saying those words about Jesus Christ to a friend, you feel a little like I did on the edge of the ledge. Be assured that you are not alone. And know that no one is behind you ready to push you before you're ready. This book will help you come to the point in your own life where you are ready to take the plunge. Be prepared to have your attitudes challenged, some of your fears put aside, and to learn some specific skills that will help you confidently share your faith.

Acknowledgments

A special thanks goes to the General NYI Council and the NYI Ministries staff for their input into this book and other products that go with the theme: Dare to Run with Vision. Janice J. Greeno deserves many kudos for all her editorial assistance and design work. Much appreciation also goes to Beverly Burgess, David Felter, Karen DeSollar, and Jeanette Gardner for the material in chapter 6.

—*Mark Gilroy*

1

Caring Means Sharing

The Motivation for Witnessing

Gary Sivewright

> *The reason that more of us don't share our faith couldn't be because we don't care, could it? All of us who claim to be saved by Jesus Christ have a great desire to see our friends meet Him too, don't we? In this chapter, Gary Sivewright will tell you about some teens who did share their faith with friends—and why they did it. Be ready to ask yourself the tough question: Do I care enough to share?*

Kate and Leslie

Kate started coming to church because Leslie invited her. She enjoyed the parties, the Sunday night afterglows, and even an occasional Wednesday night Bible study. When we announced a teen winter ski trip, it seemed natural for Leslie to invite Kate and for Kate to accept. Our church ski trips were not what you would call high-intensity evangelism. They were fun, nobody slept, we skied our brains out, we froze our toes off, and we had a great time. Every evening the whole group would gather in the hotel's meeting room for a short devotional and some small-group response. There was no pressure, just honest sharing, and when it was all over we felt good about being together as a youth group, and we felt a little closer to the Lord. It was a good way to end an exhausting day.

I have found that skiing brings out the true colors of a youth group. Friendships are often put to the test. In fact, nothing can dissolve a friendship much faster than one experienced skier friend taking a beginning skier friend to the top of Mount No Return, and leaving him there. You want to talk about stress? Friendships go through some serious strain when one goes down the mountain sitting down while the other laughs the whole way, or worse yet, leaves him for dead on some ski trail.

On the other hand, greater love has no friend than for an experienced skier to stay with his beginning skier friend. Every learning skier needs someone to encourage him and to show patience. It means a lot for one to say, "You can do it!"—and it teaches a lot about the Body of Christ. Ski trips, much like mission trips, service projects, choir tours, retreats, etc., press us to our limits and allow time for interpersonal relationships to grow. When our ski trip came to a close, Kate was pretty well convinced as to what the church was all about. She had a good idea about the demands of Jesus on lives as she had seen the members of the youth group take the Word, apply it to their lives, and share the love of Christ with others around them.

I'd like to say Kate received Christ in a small-group Bible study after a day of skiing in the beautiful Rocky Mountains, but it didn't happen that way. Instead, we got back and life went on as usual. Except one day after school Kate was over at Leslie's house. From what I understand Kate said something like this:

"Leslie, I've been watching you for some time. You and the people at your church are different. I don't know what it is, but I want it."

Leslie proceeded to tell Kate not about an "it" but about a personal relationship with Jesus Christ. And with tears streaming down their cheeks, Kate asked the Lord into her life while sitting in Leslie's bedroom.

Randy and Barry

Randy came to church to play football. His good friend Barry was putting a team together for a church teen touch football league, so he invited Randy to be on his team's roster. The league ran like most other church sports leagues, parents yelling at the refs, players yelling at the coach, and the senior pastor yelling at the youth minister about "getting control" of the church's sports program.

After football, there was basketball, after basketball, there was softball, and it seemed like there was no shortage of opportunities for Barry to say to Randy, "Let's play ball." The great thing about Barry was his consistent witness for Christ by the way he lived. Jesus was not only a part of the way he played sports but a part of everything he did. His life-style did not go unnoticed by Randy. When Barry made friends, he introduced them to all the loves of his life—his mom's cooking, his sports, his church youth group, and his Lord. And it wasn't long before Randy was asking, "Why can't I have a life like Barry's?" Using Barry's life as a living testimony, Randy soon discovered he could trust Christ just like his friend. Before God was done, Randy influenced his brother, his mom, and his dad to become Christians. It all started with a teen believer living a consistent life in front of his friend and inviting him into a fellowship by appealing to his natural interests.

Why did they do it?

What prompted Leslie and Barry to share their faith with their friends? Was it the emphasis of a Wednesday night Bible study or a brand-new book on evangelism that got them started? Before answering for Leslie and Barry we need to ask ourselves the same

question: What is our motivation to tell others about Christ? Why should we do it?

The Bible gives us many examples of people bringing people to Jesus (John 1:41). We are told by Christ to be witnesses (Acts 1:8). We look around at our world, and we see a hopeless void that cannot be filled by things and people. When we see people hurting or lonely, we want to do something. Even when we see friends filling their lives with things that at best are selfish and self-serving, and at worst are self-destructive, we want to do something.

Evangelism, at its best, then, is a heart overflowing for what Christ has done for us as individuals. It is a response much like that of Peter's and John's when they faced the Sanhedrin, "We cannot help speaking about what we have seen and heard" (Acts 4:20).

Few become great evangelists overnight. For many it becomes a growing awareness that within them is a need to share the greatest thing that has ever happened with someone who will listen. One person said it's like one beggar telling another beggar where to find bread. It is the sense to know that you cannot make the decision to follow Christ for anyone else but yourself, but you can do everything within your power to love him into the Kingdom.

Janice

Janice didn't have many friends. Her dad worked long hours as a police officer; her mom committed suicide her senior year of high school. Often we would spend time talking about life goals, evaluating her family situation, and we would laugh a little. I would talk about Christ but felt we never made a lot of spiritual progress. Maybe she was too emotionally shaken. Maybe I wasn't direct enough. All I know is we spent a lot of time talking.

Janice graduated and I moved, and I did not see her or communicate with her for some 15 years. One day a letter showed up in my office from Janice. Since the last time I saw her, life had been a living hell. She had joined the army, got married, had a child, got divorced, tried drugs, tried to commit suicide, had her child taken away from her, and had come to the end of her rope.

She found her way back to emotional health and to the Lord by making her way back to the church that had always loved her. In the letter she paid me the evangelistic dividend on a 15-year investment. "I remember our talks. You cared. You made me laugh. I just wanted to tell you you made a difference in my life."

I like to think it came from the overflow of my heart.

To Think About, to Discuss, and to Do . . .

1. Read 2 Cor. 5:11-21. What compelled Paul to become an ambassador of Jesus Christ to the world?

2. If you asked Leslie and Barry what motivated them to share their faith with friends, how do you think each would answer?

3. Rate your motivation level to share your faith with your friends. What increases your motivation? What decreases your motivation?

4. Pray that the Lord will give you a burden of love for your friends who are hurting, who are lonely, who have a void in their lives that only Jesus can fill.

5. On the left side of a sheet of paper, write down the names of five friends who do not know Jesus Christ. Across from each name, in a middle column, write out the way(s) that this person demonstrates his need for Jesus Christ. In the right column, write a prayer for all your friends, that the Holy Spirit would guide you as to the right time, place, and way to share your faith with one or more friends. Save this list while you work through the rest of the book.

Gary Sivewright is a popular speaker who has spoken to thousands of teens both nationally and internationally. A youth author, his latest book is Still Following. *He is the director of Youth Ministries for the Church of the Nazarene.*

2

Go When God Says Go

A Biblical Example of Evangelism

Gary Sivewright

> Maybe you're thinking, *Even if I want to share my faith, I just don't have the confidence to go out and tell someone else about it. It is definitely a risky idea. My friends might not be interested. It might not work out anyway.* Well, don't give up yet. This book will give you many how-tos for sharing your faith. And in this chapter, Gary Sivewright will give you a quick sketch of how one biblical character went about witnessing. You still may not feel comfortable with the idea of sharing your faith, but perhaps after hearing Philip's story, you will be more confident!

"Head south, young man . . ."

One of the best biblical examples of an evangelistic confrontation is found in Acts 8. Philip was part of the inner circle of believers in Jerusalem when he was told by an angel to head south on a desert road that led to Gaza (v. 26). Christians were persecuted in Jerusalem, but let's not downplay the difficulty of leaving the warm fellowship of family and friends. Remember, Philip was with the apostles. He was right there at the heart of the Early Church.

Those of us who have grown up in the church understand the comfort that comes by being around those who have experienced the same spiritual awakening and growth as we have. Like the afterglow following an exciting Sunday evening church service, or the bus ride home after a particularly meaningful retreat or camp, we really never want the feeling to end. One way to keep that feeling is to linger in the presence of those who share the experience. But an angel of the Lord told Philip to go. We are not told of any struggle or regret. The writer Luke simply says, "So he started out" (8:27).

Go when God says go

Lesson number one seems clear here—when God tells you to go, go. Seldom will you find people who desperately need Christ in the friendly confines of your home church. This is not to downplay the importance of church involvement. There is much to be said about the building up of the Body (see Eph. 4:12), which should encourage us to minister to each other with the gifts that God has given us. One of these gifts is evangelism (4:11), leading some to believe that only those who have the "gift" of leading others to Jesus should respond to a call like Philip's. But all who claim the name of Christ have been called to "go." This means looking in places that aren't as comfortable as our pew at church.

When I was first trained to share my faith in Christ, I was taken to Los Angeles International Airport where I was dropped off with 40 other "evangelists" loaded down with religious surveys as discussion starters and *Four Spiritual Laws* booklets. The idea was to find someone who would take the time to answer the survey questions. The questions would allow the person giving the survey to testify and share the *Four Spiritual Laws* (a gospel tract developed by Campus Crusade for Christ). I remember being scared to death, so I asked a friend who was to be my witnessing partner, "What should we do?" His sage advice was pure and simple. "Let's go to the bathroom!" At that point in my evangelistic career that sounded like an excellent idea. We made our way to the rest room. You can imagine our surprise when we discovered all the other evangelism trainees assigned to the airport that day washing their hands in the same bathroom. After about 20 minutes, it seemed that LAX's washroom would not be the best place to confront people about Christ, so I set out on my own. It's strange that though I was in the middle of one of the world's busiest airports, I could not find anyone to talk to. It's not that they weren't there, there were people everywhere. But I was out of my "comfort zone," and there was a real fear of being rejected.

I finally decided I had to do something. I chose as my target a boy sitting by himself on a long row of seats. (I picked him because he was smaller than me and probably wouldn't try to punch my face in!) I found out he was a junior high student from Oklahoma City, on vacation with his family in southern California. I asked him if he would mind taking a religious survey. He said he had time to kill. We finished the survey and went right into the *Four Spiritual Laws*. At the end of the booklet are two circles, one depicting sin in a person's life and the other representing Christ in a person's life. I said, "Jason, which circle represents your life right now?" He pointed to the circle depicting sin. I then asked, "What circle would you like to have represent your life?" He pointed to the circle with Christ in the middle. I said, "There's a prayer here in the booklet that asks Jesus to come into our lives. You wouldn't want to pray that prayer, would you?" Jason said yes. And the very first person I ever confronted with the gospel one-to-one prayed with me to receive Christ in Los Angeles International Airport! It wasn't pretty, and it didn't go all that smoothly, but God convinced me that afternoon that there are many people waiting to hear about Jesus and the difference He can make. We must be willing to go and find them.

Find out where they are

After finding them, probably outside the walls of our church,

we must discover the kind of people they are. The Bible does not tell us what Philip might have had in common with an Ethiopian eunuch who possessed enough political and financial clout to have his own private chariot. It seems not unlike you or me approaching a Madison Avenue high roller sitting in a big limousine in New York City—highly impossible. But the evangelist's common ground was what the Ethiopian was looking at. Hearing him read aloud from the prophet Isaiah, Philip approached the chariot and asked a great leading question—"Do you understand what you are reading?" (v. 30).

"How can I . . . unless someone explains it to me?" (v. 31), replied the man. What an opening! Lesson number two—find out where they are. That means you listen for the questions:

"Why is this happening to me?" "Why are you so happy all the time?" "Doesn't that make you mad?" "Why don't you try it?"

All these questions can lead to some very important answers, and we don't even have to manipulate the conversation. The questions tell us where people are.

A while back I was talking to a minister friend about the latest trends in the youth culture. One of the more shocking discoveries is that many teens in the church see nothing wrong with having premarital sexual intercourse. In fact, 20% to 25% have had such a relationship before they graduate from high school. His reply was, "They need to know that sex before marriage is sin, and sin will send them to hell." I didn't have the heart to tell him he was wrong. I don't want to discount the power of sin, nor do I want to minimize the fact that the wages of sin is death (hell), but I don't believe that is a message that will make much difference for the youth of the '90s.

Parents are bailing out on their children by such a rate that some have said 90% of the children will have experienced a single-parent relationship before the end of this century. Teenage pregnancy is happening every 30 seconds in the U.S., most out of wedlock.[1] Suicide among the young results in a successful attempt every four hours[2]—only God knows how many try and fail. Those of us who speak at camps and retreats are familiar with the statistic that as many as 25% of the young ladies there have been abused physically, sexually, or verbally.[3] A lesser percentage of the young men also fall into the category. Listen to the questions teens are asking—Is there any hope? Does anybody care? That will tell you where they are.

Tell them about Jesus

In the hopeless world of today's young people comes hope in Christ. "Then Philip began with that very passage of Scripture and told him the good news about Jesus" (v. 35). Even if it seems that their greatest problem is what to wear to school, making the team, or getting a date for Friday night, the answer for any young person who must eventually come to grips with the meaning of life is Christ.

We trained one girl how to share her faith by simply asking questions of people she would meet. She had a natural ability to make friends, but she was skeptical about people wanting to talk about religious things. I gave her a lead question. "Do you ever feel the need for a more personal religious faith?" I told her that if a person responded negatively, she could say that she had once felt that way herself but found a personal faith in Christ, and then she could share her testimony. If the person answered that he did feel the need for a more personal religious faith, she could say that she had once felt that way herself but found that personal faith in Christ and share her testimony. No matter how the person answered, he was assured of hearing her testimony. So she tried it but was not really convinced it would work.

The first person she confronted was a Muslim girl who hated the church and hated Christians. When Diane told her she was from the church, and was a Christian, the girl went nuts. She went on and on about churches that had gone bad and church members that were hypocrites. Diane just listened, thinking all along she should have never gotten into this. When the Muslim girl was through with her tirade, Diane had little to say. "I don't know what your experiences have been like, but I feel I need to tell you that when I allowed Jesus Christ to come into my life everything turned right side up. He has made all the difference in the world." Notice that she did not defend her church, though her church was important to her. She did not recommend herself, even though she was a dynamic Christian. Diane followed the example of Philip and told the Muslim girl the good news about Jesus.

I have found there are people who do have some problems with the church. They are suspicious of people who set themselves up as examples, but I've yet to find a person that can find fault with Jesus. In fact, the difficulties people that I've come into contact with have had with Christ have been in seeing Jesus misrepresented.

This had been done by some greedy, selfish people who claim to be Christians or by well-meaning believers who just did not know how to communicate the Good News. And the good news is He can change everyone's life who trusts Him.

Follow through

Notice that after the Ethiopian said he believed, they stopped the chariot and he and Philip went down into the water for a baptism service (vv. 36-39). This could be a great case for the baptism of believers, but I don't believe this is the real lesson learned. To follow through is what Philip teaches us in his dealing with the treasurer from Ethiopia. He didn't just present the gospel and leave. In fact, there are some who believe that Philip's encounter with this influential man was so transforming that the treasurer went home and began the Christian church in his home country.

Leslie and Barry

Leslie and Barry (you met them in chapter 1) are beautiful examples of two who plugged into this biblical model. They were obedient to "go" and meet Kate and Randy where they were. Through friendship Leslie and Barry took the time to find out where they were in their lives. When the time was right, they shared the good news of Jesus with them. And they followed through. They remained friends with Randy and Kate long after they accepted Jesus as Savior. Their consistent Christian lives paid off as prime examples for Randy, Kate, and others to follow.

1. Elizabeth Stack, "Young, Innocent, and Pregnant," *Psychology Today* (October 1986), 78.

2. Fern Eckman, "Teen Suicide," *McCall's* (October 1987), 71-74.

3. Donald P. Orr and Maureen C. Downes, "Self-Concept of Adolescent Sexual Abuse Victims," *Journal of Youth and Adolescence* (October 1985), 401-10.

To Think About, to Discuss, and to Do . . .

1. When you read Acts 8:26-40, what do you think is the most amazing feature of the story?

2. As you think of the main points of the chapter, what is the hardest aspect of evangelism for you to embrace?

3. Has there ever been a natural opportunity for you to share your Christian faith with a friend? How did you respond?

4. Look through the list of five friends that you created at the end of chapter 1. Make maps of the physical locations you will need to "go" to in order to have the best opportunity to reach each one.

5. Conduct an interview at school or in another setting, asking the question, "What is the greatest need in your life right now?" This can be done verbally or written confidentially on a note card. Use the responses to help you know where your peers are coming from.

To Think About to Discuss and to Do

1. When was read A is tagged... that do you think is the most important part of the story.

... Ask in front of the room will... is... Do you not... write in the fewest pages of information that you to announce

... has third can have a natural explanation for her to your ... Classroom is help with a new of how do you respond

2. Look at the pictures of five friends over you decided at the end of the story. Make major of the practical locations not will need to go in, in order to know the past by getting only between ...

3. Conduct an interview with about... for another among asking the question "What sort thing came to mind in you. Its right now." This can be done verbally in written could in thin tape, and Let the response... help. You know where your mind are drawing from.

19

3

Do I Have to Lose My Friends to Win Them?

Finding the Right Time to Witness

Kathy Lewis

> "But some people aren't even open to receiving Jesus Christ. Is it possible to get them to think about God without really turning them off? Are there ever times when it's not the right thing to share my faith?"
>
> You'll find the answer to these and other questions in this chapter. Kathy Lewis will help you know when it is right to share your faith ... and maybe when it is not time. She will also help you see that evangelism is more than the moment that you verbally testify to someone, but a whole process of leading others closer to God. Don't miss the steps a person goes through to make a decision for Jesus Christ.

Does it have to be so unnatural?

Maybe you're like me. When you hear the term *evangelism*, a sick feeling begins to rise in your stomach. It's so awkward and aggressive and unnatural. Does God really want us to lose our friends in order to win them?

Evangelism that I have been around has often been uncomfortable. I could never quite bring myself to throw a tract at a stranger on the bus who wasn't interested! I'm not sure I could have shared with Jason like Gary did in Los Angeles International Airport (chapter 2). And I wasn't about to invite my friends to hear a pulpit-pounding evangelist who came to our church sporting an obvious toupee for their very first visit to church. Get real!

My negative attitudes toward evangelism developed primarily because I didn't know what evangelism was. As I learned more about what evangelism was and what it was not, I learned that maybe I could evangelize without losing all my friends and without the awkwardness. I learned that evangelism could become an exciting part of my life!

In this chapter we will look at what evangelism is and is not. To start the process, think for a moment what you like least about the idea of evangelism or a negative stereotype you hold. Write it in the space below. As you read this chapter, I hope that you'll find that the thing you like the least is not part of what evangelism is essentially about.

_____

_____

_____

_____

What evangelism is

Evangelism can be summed up in three parts. Evangelism is (1) aiming at making disciples, while (2) bringing the people around us closer to God, through (3) naturally communicating our faith.

Making disciples, not just decisions

As a child and as a teen, growing up in the church, I made a lot of trips down to the altar. The trouble was that on most of those trips I wasn't ready to make a decision that meant anything. I was just feeling a stirring in my heart to know more about God. I spent a lot of time feeling defeated spiritually about my constant trips to the altar because no one helped me understand that my walk with God was a process. The altar was all I knew about getting closer to God. Since my trip to the altar hadn't worked, I supposed it was because I hadn't said the right words or made a firm enough decision.

In our attempts at evangelism, sometimes we put a heavy emphasis on making a decision for Christ. That certainly isn't bad, but it can be misleading. We have come to equate evangelism with a spiritual decision, often made at an altar. However, the spiritual decision or the moment of accepting Christ as Savior is only one part of evangelism.

Now I can just hear you saying, "What does this writer mean? Isn't our ultimate goal to have people accept Christ as their Savior?" You may be surprised by my answer. The answer is "No." Our goal is not ultimately to have people accept Christ, though that is a necessary part of the goal. Jesus set our ultimate goal for us when He said, "Go and make disciples of all nations" (Matt. 28:19).

A disciple is a follower. It's a person who has chosen to follow Jesus and who continues to follow Him on a daily basis. If we get people to an altar or if we get them to pray a sinner's prayer after our presentation of the gospel, we have not necessarily introduced them to what it means to be a disciple.

To evangelize our friends in a way that will teach them to be disciples means that we must be concerned with much more than getting them to make a decision. Evangelism continues after the point of a decision. It also begins well before the point of decision. Not all of our friends are at a place where they are ready to accept Christ, but every one of our friends can learn something from us that will bring them closer to knowing God personally.

Bringing people closer to God

The spiritual decision process begins before a person even hears about God and continues until that person is a disciple who is helping other people get closer to God.

To help us understand what the spiritual decision process is, let's look at Marcos' decision about college.

Marcos

Marcos hated the thought of going to college. He hadn't ever liked school, and he couldn't bear the thought of four more years of it. Naturally, he wasn't very interested in visits from college representatives, and his guidance counselor couldn't get him to sign up for college preparatory classes. When he was invited to a seminar on financial aid, he simply refused to go.

Then Marcos met Mr. Diaz, a friend of his father. Mr. Diaz was an architect. He showed Marcos some blueprints he had created

and took him to see some of his finished buildings. Marcos had always loved to draw, and the thought of being an architect appealed to him. He decided that he would like to be one someday. However, architects, according to Mr. Diaz, had to have bachelor's degrees. Suddenly, Marcos had a new interest in college.

Now when college representatives visited Marcos' school, he was usually first in line to find out about their program in architecture. He sent away for catalogs. As he read about the programs, he found that his attitude was changing about college. He wanted to attend.

One day as Marcos was reading a university catalog, he came across the fine print that listed admissions requirements. He learned that admission to the architecture program required four years of high school math, including the college preparatory classes he had avoided. Marcos suddenly realized that his dream wouldn't be possible unless he made a change. He made an appointment with the guidance counselor to have his class schedule changed.

The spiritual decision process

The spiritual decision process is much like Marcos' decision process about college. James Engel describes this process as having seven steps.

1. Need activation
2. Search for information
3. Change in beliefs and attitudes
4. Problem recognition
5. Decision and rebirth
6. Postdecision evaluation
7. Spiritual growth

1. *Need activation.* At first, Marcos didn't see the need for college. He wasn't ready to make a decision to go. His sense of need was activated when he found out he needed college to be an architect, something he really wanted to be.

Many of our friends may be at this very first stage of the spiritual decision process. They don't see any need for Christ in their lives. They may not see that need until something painful happens to them or until they see something different in you that they want to have.

2. *Search for information.* Marcos began to search out information on colleges and universities. He still hadn't made a decision about going, but he was finding out all he could.

Some of your friends may be at a stage where they are finding out about who Christ really is. They may not be searching noticeably for information on Christ, but they are gathering data about Him. One of the main ways they do this is by watching you.

3. *Change in beliefs and attitudes.* Marcos found his opinion changing as he gathered more information about colleges. He suddenly wanted to go to college.

In the process of learning more about Christ, your friends may decide that believing in God is not as ridiculous as they once thought. They may change their attitude about what God is like. Perhaps they've always thought of God as distant and impersonal, but as they watch your life, they find that He can be a personal Friend.

4. *Problem recognition.* When Marcos gathered enough information, he saw that he had a choice to make. If he continued in his present class schedule, he could not go to college for architecture.

Your friends will eventually come to the point where they realize two things: (1) Only those who accept Christ into their hearts will have eternal life; and (2) They have not accepted Christ into their hearts. This is a crucial part of the process. It may take a while for your friends to admit that they are sinners who need God. Only after they acknowledge this are they ready for the next step.

5. *Decision and rebirth.* Marcos decided to change his schedule. Of course, this is nothing like being born again, but he did make a decision that reversed his previous direction.

That is what happens in the spiritual decision process. This is the step where people are "saved." They confess their sins and accept Christ into their lives. They reverse their previous direction in life to go God's way.

You can see that a lot of things must happen before a person is ready to make this decision. However, often we focus all of our evangelistic efforts on this one part of the process.

6. *Postdecision evaluation.* We can assume that Marcos probably had some second thoughts once he got into his harder classes. After we make any decision, we usually experience some doubts as we adjust to the idea of what has happened.

In the spiritual decision process, a person who has recently accepted Christ may also question what has just happened to him. He may have doubts or questions. He may wonder if his prayer "worked." During this time, a person needs to learn about the assurance Christ offers that our sins are forgiven.

7. *Spiritual growth.* If Marcos wanted to become an architect, he had to go on to apply to colleges, attend classes, graduate, and set up his business.

In the same way, the decision to accept Christ is only the beginning. The disciple who wants to grow in the Lord must become involved in the local church, worship regularly, have daily quiet times with God, become a good steward of talents and money, and accept the challenge to make other disciples.

Tony

See if you can identify the stages of the spiritual decision process in the life of Tony. Write them in the margin as you read through his story.

Tony wasn't a bad kid. He didn't do drugs, and he didn't drink. He was an athlete, and he tried to keep away from things that would compromise his health. Tony even hung around the church some. His friend Andrea had invited him, and he had started to come occasionally to youth group events. He especially liked the gym nights they had once a month.

However, Tony wasn't a Christian. He wouldn't have been upset if you asked him, but he would have told you no. He thought Christianity was just fine for some people, and he even had a lot of friends who were Christians, but he didn't see a need for God in his life.

26

Then Tony's teammate Ray was killed in a car wreck on the way back from the state basketball tournament. Tony couldn't believe it. He began to withdraw. He stopped going to church. He was mad at God. He had big questions about a God that would allow his friend to be senselessly killed.

One afternoon, Pastor Loren came to see Tony. He stopped by to watch basketball practice and asked if he could take Tony for a Coke. Tony accepted. He thought Pastor Loren would give him some straight answers to his questions about God. So over a Coke, Tony fired questions at him for at least an hour. Pastor Loren suggested some scriptures for Tony to read and invited him to begin attending a weekly Bible study with two other guys his age, Scott and Roger. Surprisingly, Tony agreed.

Over the next three months, Tony searched. Each week he brought his questions to Scott and Roger, and they helped him find answers in the Bible. Tony began to see that God is a loving Father. He allows painful things to happen because they bring about ultimate good. There is evil and pain in the world because God gave man a choice, and man chose evil. Tony began to see that he, too, had a choice about whether or not to accept Christ.

One night as they walked home from Bible study, Tony asked Roger to help him pray to receive Christ. In the days that followed, Pastor Loren discipled Tony. He helped Tony understand the implications of what he had decided. Tony eventually became a leader in his youth group. He even began to share with his friends on the basketball team about Jesus Christ.

Who was the evangelist in this story? Was it Roger, or Scott, or Pastor Loren, or Andrea, the girl who first invited him to church? The answer is "yes" to all of the above. Each of these people took the time to find out where Tony was in his spiritual decision process, and they did what was necessary to bring him closer to God. Roger was the one who actually prayed with Tony, but all of them helped evangelize Tony. Evangelism is bringing people closer to God.

Naturally communicating my faith

A final point that we need to make in our definition of evangelism is that evangelism is natural communication. By that we don't mean that it comes naturally. Evangelism is hard work and requires a lot of preparation. But when it comes to sharing our faith with our friends, it is just that—friendly sharing. We aren't trying to trap anyone. When we try to trap our friends we usually trip them instead. We make everyone uncomfortable, and we may succeed in turning our friends off to Christ rather than winning them.

In evangelism, our words and our nonverbal messages must match. If we can't be real people when we share our faith, our friends won't believe our faith is something real. We will be talking more about how to make our sharing natural in the next few chapters.

It may help you be more natural if you learn a gospel presentation or use a tract. However, if you are more concerned with what you have planned to say than really sharing with the person, you may not want to use either.

Summary

Evangelism is me living my life in such a way that I draw my friends into wanting to know more about God. To do this I must recognize that not all of my friends are ready to make a decision for Jesus. I can be an evangelist by being a good friend, finding out where my friends are in the spiritual decision process, and helping them move closer to God by naturally communicating my faith in my everyday interactions with them.

To Think About, to Discuss, and to Do...

1. Read 1 Cor. 3:1-9. How were Paul and Apollos different as evangelists? Which do you most identify with?

2. What is the difference between having as your ultimate goal getting people saved or making disciples?

3. What did you list as the thing you like the least about the idea of evangelism? What have you learned from this chapter that has changed your idea of evangelism? In your own words, how would you define evangelism after reading this chapter?

4. Think of two of your friends who are not Christians. On the spiritual decision chart on page 30, try to identify the stage where they are. Mark the stage with an X and write the person's initials beside it.

5. For each friend listed on page 30, what one question might be on his mind at his present stage on the spiritual decision process?

6. Think back about how you became a Christian. Use the "Spiritual Decision Process" and write out what happened to you at each step.

Kathy Lewis is youth minister at the Pasadena, Calif., Bresee Avenue Church of the Nazarene. She is also a free-lance writer and was formerly a youth curriculum editor for WordAction Publishing Company.

SPIRITUAL DECISION CHART
1. NEED ACTIVATION
2. SEARCH FOR INFORMATION
3. CHANGE IN BELIEFS AND ATTITUDES
4. PROBLEM RECOGNITION
5. DECISION AND REBIRTH
6. POSTDECISION EVALUATION
7. SPIRITUAL GROWTH

4

What *Difference* Does Being *Different* Make?

Life-style Evangelism

Susie Shellenberger

Could it be that one reason we don't have opportunities to share our faith is we really aren't much different from non-Christians? I'm not talking about being different to be weird but different in the ways that really count. Like how we treat others. In this chapter Susie Shellenberger will describe one person who practiced life-style evangelism. Deron's life spoke volumes. As you read this chapter let the Spirit convict you of areas in your life that need to be different.

A dramatic victory

The air inside South Oak's gymnasium was filled with a mixture of sweat, popcorn, and uncontrolled exhilaration. Less than a minute remained in the last game of the season. The players couldn't even hear Coach Martin's blaring instructions from the sidelines, the roar of the student body was so loud.

The band played the familiar school fight song while eight

energetic cheerleaders led the crowd in audible support. South Oak High School trailed by one, and two of the first-string players had fouled out earlier in the game.

The opposing team called a time-out, and Coach Martin grabbed Deron. "Get the ball to Alex as quickly as you can. It's not too late! We can still pull this one off."

Deron and Alex were a team within a team. Watching the two high school juniors on the basketball court was like watching poetry in motion. They always seemed to be a step ahead of the rest of the players. They passed the ball around, but it was obvious they had more ability than anyone else on the entire first string. It was no wonder now, when every second counted, that Coach Martin tossed teamwork out the window and encouraged them to "do their thing."

The buzzer sounded and the game was in motion once again. The opposing team started down the court with the ball. Coach Martin yelled from the sidelines. Deron stabbed for the ball with his lightning reflexes and miraculously stole it from the befuddled Eagle guard. Almost as if he had read Deron's mind, Alex was already headed down the court for their goal.

With eight seconds left on the clock, Deron swished past two guards and passed straight to Alex, now under the basket with two seconds remaining. With one motion, Alex caught the pass and rammed the ball through the hoop as the final buzzer sounded South Oak's dramatic victory!

Almost immediately the team was mobbed with friends, family members, and local newspaper sports photographers.

"Let's celebrate!" Mike yelled to his teammates as he rolled on the gym floor."

"Let's party!" joined Alex.

The locker room buzzed with plans for the night.

"Who's grabbing the 'brew'?"

"My older brother's meeting us at Kwik Stop in half an hour. He said if we won tonight, the first three six-packs are on him," announced Chad.

"All right!"

"What a brother!"

"Yeah, and he also said if we'll meet him outside the store with our money, he'll get everything else we want."

"What are we waiting for? Let's get out of here!"

"Yeah! We got some serious partying to do!"

"Hey, Deron! Why don't you make an exception and come with us this time?" invited Mike.

"Yeah, Deron! Really be part of the team this time," pressed Alex.

"C'mon, guys, you know I don't drink."

"So what? Just come and have fun with the rest of us. You don't have to drink," Alex continued.

"I can think of better things to do than watching you guys fall all over each other." Deron laughed. "You can tell me all about it on Monday . . . the part you're able to recall. Catch you later!"

Deron waited until Saturday afternoon to give Alex a call. "How you doing, Al?"

"Uhhh," he moaned. "Can you come over? I want to talk."

"Sure, but it doesn't sound like you're in the best of shape right now. Are you sure this is a good time?"

"No, it's not a good time, but I want to talk to you anyway. Please, Deron. Just come over."

Deron placed the receiver in its cradle and headed toward Alex's. He couldn't help focusing on the memories they'd shared during the past five years. He smiled as he recalled their first meeting on the baseball field in the Blue Tigers Little League. Alex had his cap on backward, his symbol of doing things "his way." They had collided during practice, when both were going for a fly ball. Even though their white practice pants were covered with dirt and grass stains, the boys laughed hysterically and began a close friendship.

The following year, Alex's family moved into a neighborhood in Deron's school district, and the two had become even closer. Though Alex sometimes accepted his invitation to attend church, Deron was still praying for his salvation.

As he turned the corner to drive the last five blocks to Downing Street, he remembered how close Alex had been to making a spiritual decision last summer when he had agreed to attend church camp. Though he was desperately interested in knowing God better, it was obvious something was still holding him back.

Now, as they were in the middle of their junior year, Deron worried that he was completely losing Alex to the party scene. It had become a Friday night ritual for the rest of the team to get drunk after every game—whether they won or not. Alex had fallen prey to the pressure.

As he shut the car door and climbed the porch steps, Deron wondered what he could say this time that he hadn't already said before.

He found Alex in his bedroom with the curtains drawn and the lights off, obviously experiencing a wicked hangover. Deron sat on the floor beside the bed and spoke softly.

"You look awful!"

"Tell me about it," Alex agreed. "Someone slipped some 'X' in my drink last night. Ohhh. My insides feel like they've been ripped apart with a lawn mower."

Deron didn't know a lot about "X," other than the fact it was short for "ecstasy" and was a powerful and popular new drug making the rounds at his high school. "Alex, do you really think it's worth it? I mean, look at you!"

"That's what I want to talk to you about. Deron, I've known you for a long time, pal. No matter how many times I've screwed up my life, you've remained a real friend."

"Hey, listen . . ."

"No. You listen! I know I'm not in real good shape right now, but I do know what I'm talking about. You've always been so together. The only reason I started partying was because I couldn't say no to the pressure. I just wanted to be included, you know?"

"I hear you."

"But, you never gave in. Everyone knows what you stand for; they all know about God being in your life and all that. Everyone knows how involved you are in your church and youth group. And the times I've gone with you, I've really enjoyed it. I've come real close several times to making a commitment to God, but something always holds me back."

"I know. I've sensed that."

"I want what you have, Deron. I need that strength. I don't want to keep giving in to the pressure of things that I really don't even want to do. I want what you have!"

"Alex, that's great!" Deron yelled. Then he remembered, as Alex covered his ears and winced in pain, that he needed to keep his volume in control.

"Hold on," Alex continued. "I want to give my life to Christ, but I'm scared. Don't tell anybody I said that!"

"C'mon, Al! I'm your friend, remember?"

"Yeah, yeah. I guess I'm just scared of all I know I'll have to give up to become a Christian."

"Listen to me," Deron began. "All the things you'll give up to follow the Lord and go to heaven are the very same things that are ruining your life and that you really don't want anyway. You said it yourself."

When Alex didn't say anything, Deron continued, "It just makes sense to give your life to God. It's obvious you're miserable. You already said you need God's strength to say no to the things you don't want to do."

"Yeah, I know," Alex agreed.

"But you're right in knowing the cost," Deron continued. "Following Jesus isn't always easy. It means saying no to some attractive things everyone else seems to be doing. And they'll probably give you a hard time about it too. But, hey, look who God's blessed you with for a friend?"

"Get off it!" Alex smiled, as he tossed a pillow at Deron's head. "Everything you're saying makes a lot of sense. I'm still scared, but I really want to do this. I need to do this!"

Deron smiled and breathed a prayer for help as he leaned forward and pulled his pocket-sized New Testament out of his hip pocket.

Life-style evangelism

Deron's life-style had opened the door for Alex's salvation. Within his life-style, he also held three important aspects of leading someone to Christ. Let's take a brief glance at Deron's secrets. Notice that life-style evangelism for him meant . . .

1. *Friendship*. By being a friend to Alex, Deron had earned the right to be heard. He had taken the time to establish rapport. Their friendship spanned five years. They had shared baseball, basketball, camping, and several other common interests. By simply being a friend to Alex over the years, he had earned his respect and won his trust.

Focus on the things you and your non-Christian friend share in common. You can be a friend by being an encourager. If your common interest is sports, encourage your friend in this specific area. Affirm him. Take the time to build him up. Help him feel confident around you. This will enhance the process of building trust and rapport.

2. *Consistency*. Deron was consistent. First of all, he was consistent in his friendship with Alex. He continued to encourage him and kept the lines of communication open, even when Alex drifted into other areas. He wasn't condemning, yet he clearly didn't condone Alex's actions either.

Chances are, your non-Christian friend already knows what's wrong in his life. Instead of trying to focus on the wrongs, continue to love him and make it clear you want him involved in your youth group. Invite him often and encourage his attendance. When he does come, make him feel loved and accepted by including other church friends into his life.

Deron was also consistent in his walk with Christ. It would have been easy to accept the invitation to the party and simply not drink once he arrived. But Deron knew his impact would eventually be stronger if he didn't attend the party at all.

He took a strong stand for what he believed was right. This

made it absolutely clear in Alex's mind that compromise was not acceptable to him. Because of Deron's consistency in avoiding evil, Alex was able to better discern the difference in his life and the lives of his other friends. Obviously, he eventually came to the conclusion that he wanted that difference.

Many times Christian teens rationalize and think, It would be a good witness to attend the party and not drink. Then everyone would know I'm a Christian and could actually see me taking a stand. But the next day at school when the hallway gossip floats through the tiles and someone's naming off everyone who attended the party, they won't take the time to stop and say, "Oh yeah, but I don't think he drank anything." Your name will simply be remembered as one among many who attended the party.

What kind of witness is that? Surprise! Your non-Christian friends see it as one big inconsistency. They don't want to see how similar you can be to them; if you're claiming to be a Christian, they want to see the difference!

3. *Love*. First Corinthians 13 tells us that love is patient. Alex had come close to making a spiritual commitment several times. When he didn't make a commitment at last summer's camp, Deron may have been tempted to respond, "What is it with you, Alex? I give up." But he didn't. He continued to love and realized that giving love is patient.

It's frustrating to share your faith with your non-Christian friends, or have them attend church and youth group functions with you, and be slow on the commitment factor. But if you can consistently provide a loving example of a Christlike life-style, you'll eventually establish the right to be heard through solid rapport.

At a luncheon held at Azusa Pacific University, on February 7, 1990, Tony Campolo addressed a crowd of professors and students. Commenting on personal evangelism, he told of asking a crowd of 10,000 how they were won to the Lord.

He speculated, "When I asked how many came to know Jesus Christ through television evangelism, no one raised a hand. When I asked how many were won to the Lord through evangelistic tracts, no hands were raised. When I asked how many became Christians through radio ministry, I saw 4 hands go up. When I inquired as to how many were won through a great sermon, I counted 40 hands.

"When I finally asked, 'How many of you came to know Jesus Christ personally because someone locked on to you and wouldn't let you go?' a sea of hands all over the auditorium were raised."

What does that tell us about evangelism? When our life is truly different it will truly make a difference on those around us.

To Think About, to Discuss, and to Do . . .

1. Susie mentioned "patience." What are some other characteristics of love from 1 Corinthians 13 that will positively impact the lives of your friends?

2. What person made the biggest impact on your becoming a Christian? How would you describe this person's life-style?

3. How does the quality of your own life-style measure up in terms of friendship, consistency, and love toward others?

4. List some specific ways Christians can actively show the important differences Jesus Christ has made in their lives.

5. This will take some courage. Talk to a friend or two, and ask them to give you honest feedback on how well you demonstrate Christlikeness through your life-style. Ask them to tell you where both your strengths and your weaknesses are.

Susie Shellenberger practiced personal evangelism through her position as a staff youth minister for seven years and as a public high school teacher for four years. She is a national youth speaker and currently serves as editor of Brio *magazine published by Focus on the Family.*

5

Natural Bridges

How to Bring Up Spiritual Matters

Ed Robinson

> Why is it that preachers and evangelists always have such
> dramatic stories of people at airports who ask them if they
> know what the meaning of life is? All of us would witness if
> opportunities like that came our way! In this chapter, Dr. Ed
> Robinson gives some helpful ideas on how spiritual matters
> can be brought up naturally in the course of daily conversa-
> tions. As you read through this chapter, think of an unsaved
> friend and gather ideas on how you might raise the issue of
> his spiritual condition.

Why don't we witness?

Why don't more Christian teens (and adults for that matter)
witness to their family, friends, or anyone else who doesn't know
Jesus as personal Savior? Why do we say we are followers of Christ
and have such a difficult time giving our testimony and presenting
the gospel to non-Christians? Maybe it's because we are not really
convinced of the need; or perhaps we don't know what to say; or
maybe we just can't find any "sinners" to witness to; or maybe . . .
none of the above.

Really. Most Christians don't need to be convinced of the need to share their faith with others. We have heard enough sermons and attended enough Bible studies on the topic of evangelism to know that witnessing is an important part of what it means to be a Christian. Being convinced of the need to witness is not what keeps us from witnessing as often as we should.

For some Christians, being able to outline the plan of salvation in some logical order isn't that much of a challenge either. A good plan or tract is usually all we need. It isn't that hard to learn four or five key points with some supporting Scripture passages that add strength to the presentation. Many Christians have practiced such a presentation in a class, a workshop, or a youth group meeting. Perhaps you even know a good opening line or two from a gospel presentation: "Do you know that God loves you and has a plan for your life?" or "If you were to die tonight and come to the gates of heaven and God should ask you, 'Why should I let you into my heaven,' what would you say?" How about Rom. 3:23, John 3:16, or Rev. 3:20? Sound familiar? You see, not knowing how to explain the gospel to a person in a way that is true and sensible really isn't the reason most of us don't witness more.

Maybe the reason we don't share our faith with sinners more is that we can't find any that need salvation. Right. If your world is as normal as mine is, you know that just isn't true. Not everybody you know is a Christian; not everyone goes to church somewhere already; not everyone we know has a vital relationship with Jesus Christ. We don't really believe that everyone in our world of influence is already a believer. What we see and hear in an average day at school or in our community won't allow us to believe a naive idea like that. The reason we don't witness more often is not because we can't find anybody to witness to. Our worlds are full of people who need to hear what we have to say.

Well, if we are already convinced of the need to witness, and we can learn a presentation of the gospel that makes sense, and we know some people who need to hear the good news that Jesus died for their sins and wants to save them, why don't we witness more? What makes many of us Christians afraid to just go out there and share our faith with others?

How do you bring up the topic of spiritual matters?

I am convinced that more of us don't share our testimony

because we aren't quite sure how to bring up the topic of spiritual issues in the course of our daily conversations. We're not sure how to make the transition from talking about school, sports, or Saturday's date to talking about salvation, sin, or Satan's schemes. It's not so much that we don't have the words, the opportunity, or the desire. We just don't know how to get into a conversation about the gospel.

Most of us are not into carrying an oversized Bible to school or standing on a soapbox and preaching during the lunch hour. We can't just walk up to a person and ask, "Friend, do you know where you are going to spend eternity?" We'd feel uncomfortable moving from a discussion about dating to a presentation of the gospel by saying, "Speaking of getting ready for a date, did you know that you have a date with God's eternal judgment? Are you ready for that one?!" Not subtle ways to approach the topic.

Even a softer approach would leave a lot of us squirming in our Reeboks, "Bob, speaking of being in love with someone, did you know that God loves you and has a wonderful plan for your life." It's not that it sounds bad or insincere, it's just that it isn't natural for most of us. That's not the way we usually talk. I know there are some Christians who can have those kinds of conversations about spiritual matters as if it were the most ordinary thing in the world. Frankly, most of us just can't do that. We usually shy away from things that are unnatural or uncomfortable for us.

Natural, sincere, and from the heart

So how do you approach the topic of spiritual things in the

41

course of conversation with others so it comes out sincere, not phony; natural, not put-on; from the heart, not from a manual—or this book? If we could figure out a way to make spiritual issues a "natural" part of our conversation with others, we just might be more eager to share our faith on a more consistent (and natural) basis.

Before we get into the specifics about how to make transitions from everyday kinds of topics to spiritual things, it is important to establish a few ideas about witnessing to others.

Idea 1—Witnessing usually involves earning the right to be heard. Most people will listen to our message if they have already seen the evidence of our words in our life. When the actions of our life are inconsistent with the message we are trying to convey, we are sending what is often called a "mixed message." It is always difficult to get the true meaning of a mixed message because we know part of the message isn't correct. In most instances, we will reject the verbal message (the words) in favor of the visual message (the actions). No matter how smooth the transitions in conversations from the commonplace to the spiritual, Christians can't expect others to listen to what they have to say about Jesus if their behavior is noticeably different from their witness.

What I'm saying here is the same point Susie Shellenberger made in chapter 4. You might even want to review Susie's three main points of friendship, consistency, and love.

Being a good friend (by caring, sharing, loving, listening, and being loyal) will determine to a large degree how open others will be to the gospel we share. Developing good, quality friendships is a key to being able to bring up spiritual matters with others.

Idea 2—Witnessing involves both action (which I have mentioned already) and words. Developing the ability to carry on a conversation is important. Now you may be one of those kinds of persons who can talk with just about anybody. You can talk a mile (or a kilometer) a minute with ease. I am not one of those persons. I have to work on being able to talk with someone for more than a few grunts and few yeah-huhs. I've had to force myself to be open in conversation with others at school, in the grocery store, in the foyer at church, and just about every place except the comforts of my own living room. If we as Christians expect to share (speak) about our faith with others, we have to make a commitment to overcome the fear or discomfort of talking with others.

Idea 3—Our friends really are interested in the truths we believe and the ideas that guide our lives. Now, most of them are not interested in getting "preached at" on a regular basis, but they do want to know who we are and what makes us do the things we do. In fact, most teenagers are very interested in spiritual concerns that affect choices, ideals, life and death, and a relationship to God (the majority—about 90%—of youth in North America do believe in God). What they are not interested in is someone trying to tell them how bad they are and how much they need to go to church to get straightened out.

Somehow, we have to get over the idea that people around us are not interested in spiritual matters. We trick ourselves into believing that our friends are not interested in what we have to say, so we don't bother even trying. Getting over this misunderstanding can go a long way toward helping us approach the topic of the spiritual life with friends. If we assume that no one is interested in what we have to say about our faith, that is probably the response we'll find. But if we expect people to be interested, more than likely we'll discover that they really are.

Idea 4—We are never alone when we set out to witness. God, through His Holy Spirit, goes before, stands beside, and sticks around after we're done each time we share our faith with others. That's God's promise. It can sometimes feel like the loneliest experience of life standing in a group of non-Christians sharing our faith. But the truth is that we are never alone. The Holy Spirit is present. I have known times when the conversation I was involved in turned to spiritual things when I wasn't even looking for it. That's God's Holy Spirit at work. He is not only giving us strength to say the things we need to say but also providing the opportunities for us to say them!

Natural bridges to spiritual matters

So now, how do we get into spiritual issues when we are talking about the common events of life? Figuring out what kinds of topics lead to opportunities to share our testimony isn't really that complicated. Here are some ideas you might consider.

1. *Church involvement.* Your involvement in church activities can provide a natural bridge to spiritual matters. Toward the end of the school week, the question, "What are you doing this weekend?" is often asked. If you're doing something with the youth group at

church, say so! Many of your friends may already know that you are actively involved in the church's ministries, and they might be interested in knowing why you spend so much time there. Three possible results could follow: (1) they just might be interested in joining you for some of the activities, or (2) they might be interested in why you would invest that kind of time and energy in church activities rather than the usual party mode, or (3) they may not care a bit, in which case nothing is necessarily gained, but nothing is lost.

Perhaps a transitional phrase like, "Would you be interested in going to the church skate night with me?" could serve as an open door to a discussion about the place of church and the importance of the spiritual emphasis that is presented there. You might get some resistance since many people have already built their defenses against the hypocrisy of church people they have known. That is an outstanding opportunity then to talk about the fact the real basis of Christian faith is not in a church, or in other people, but in the person of Jesus Christ. A good way to approach this issue is to say, "You're right. I have also discovered that there are people in church who don't really live the Christian life as they should. But the basis for becoming a Christian is not church attendance. It's having a personal relationship with Christ. May I share about my relationship to Him?" The way then is open to talk about what a personal relationship with Christ really is. Your involvement in church is just the bridge to be able to talk about the important issues of the gospel.

2. *Contemporary issues.* Another good topic that can serve as an opening to talk about Christ is news related to contemporary moral problems. Many school newspapers will include editorials or news items related to moral issues (AIDS, poverty, war and peace, justice, and the death penalty, to name just a few). Sometimes, these topics are the focus of discussion in civics, history, or even health class. Use these topics as a springboard to talking about the basis on which moral choices are made. A simple question like, "What did you think about the editorial concerning AIDS in the school paper?" can serve as the launching pad for a conversation about morality, standards, and personal choice. That's *not* an invitation to argue (or to solve the problem) as much as it is an invitation to talk about your standards, your choices, and your faith. Now this will require that you have some idea on what basis you make your choices. If you are a serious follower of Jesus, your faith is going to have a significant part in that.

3. *Personal problems.* If you have established a good friendship with others, the chances are very good that someday when they are facing serious problems or difficult situations, they will confide in you. Be a good listener, but also look for the opportunity, when it arises, to talk about how faith allows you to deal with those same situations (or ones similar to them) in a constructive way.

Be careful at this point that you don't just "jump over" their problem so that you can quickly "share the gospel." Take time to listen, and allow them to talk through their concerns and cares. Then respond with your perspective about how God helps you overcome. Paul Little, in his book *How to Give Away Your Faith,** suggests using a phrase like, "You know, I used to feel like that until I had an experience that changed my outlook on life. Would you like me to tell you about it?" If you have never had a similar experience, you might respond with "You know, I might feel that way, too, except for an experience I had that changed the way I look at things." The important thing is not that you've walked in your friend's shoes. The point is the difference Christ makes in your life today!

4. *Music and media.* Music, videos, books, and TV programs can be a good tool for bridging the gap between the commonplace and the spiritual. After you've watched, read, or heard something that has some connection to things that are spiritual (either by positive or negative association), ask your friend, "What did you think about that message?" and see what develops in conversation.

You can talk about your interpretation of it from a Christian view-point and take advantage of the chance to explain why you see it that way.

If you have a Christian tape that you particularly enjoy, why not share it with a friend and ask what he thinks of the music *and* the lyrics. Sometimes the messages are very clearly Christian. With some groups, the lyrics may not be as openly Christian. Their lyrics are more subtle, providing a chance to talk about what the words really say. This can be an excellent way of getting into a topic of the spiritual life.

5. *Your life-style.* A final category that can serve as a bridge to talking about spiritual things is questions others may ask about the quality and actions of your life. There are times when your Christian faith will be expressed in situations with love instead of hate, with joy instead of sadness, with hope instead of despair, with conviction instead of compromise. Someone may observe you praying before lunch in the cafeteria or in class before an exam (hopefully, not because you haven't studied as much as you should have). You may be asked, "What makes you so happy?" or "What makes you respond like that?" or "Why do you act that way?" or "Why are you acting so different this year?" That is an open invitation to share how God has made a difference in the way you look at the situations of life.

Preparing to relax

These ideas for bridging the gap between the kinds of conversations we usually have and talking about spiritual issues are not very unique or particularly creative. You could probably think of some others I have not mentioned. But the lack of uniqueness or creativity is exactly the point. They are very natural. That's how we want our witness to be. The problem is in the fact that we are not usually prepared to respond to these situations because we have not thought about the opportunities ahead of time. We often think of the good, natural responses about an hour after the opportunity presented itself. By then it's too late.

Paul Little writes, "Knowing what we are going to say before-hand will help overcome nervousness and put us at ease. If we clutch [hesitate], the other person clutches; but if we relax, he or she relaxes." As we learn to recognize the opportunities to strike up a conversation about spiritual issues and eventually have an invitation to share our own faith and the plan of salvation with our friends, the more those opportunities will increase.

Remember, the real reason most of us Christians don't witness is not because we are not convinced of the need; or that we don't know how to talk about the plan of salvation; or that we can't find anyone who is not a Christian. The reason is that we just can't seem to figure out how to bring up the topic of the Christian life in a natural conversation with our friends. Maybe with these few ideas and potential opportunities, we can overcome that shortcoming and begin sharing our faith more consistently.

* Paul Little, *How to Give Away Your Faith* (Downers Grove, Ill.: InterVarsity Press, 1966).

To Think About, to Discuss, and to Do . . .

1. Read Acts 17:16-34. What method(s) did Paul use to bring up spiritual matters with the Athenians?

2. Which of the five methods for bringing up spiritual methods was most helpful for you? Least helpful? Explain why.

3. Think of a non-Christian friend of yours, and determine the most natural way to bring up spiritual matters with him.

4. Keep that same friend in mind and "prepare to relax." Practice in your mind how a conversation about his spiritual life might progress with that friend.

5. Keep a sheet of paper with you for the next seven days. Each time a natural opportunity to bring up spiritual matters arises, write it down—time, place, topic, people involved. Then record if you took advantage of the opportunity. Determine why you were able or unable to do so, and commit this area of your life to the Lord.

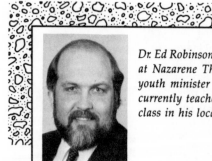

Dr. Ed Robinson is a professor of youth ministry at Nazarene Theological Seminary. He was a youth minister in California for 16 years and currently teaches a senior high Sunday School class in his local church.

6

But What Do I Say?

Four Ways to Present the Gospel to a Friend

> *OK, you have reached a point in your relationship with a friend that he is seriously interested in knowing what it means to be a Christian. What are you going to say now? This chapter provides four of the most familiar plans of sharing the gospel with a non-Christian friend. It is a little longer and will take some concentration. As you read, your challenge is to find the method that best expresses what it means to be a Christian for you.*

In the four short stories below, you will discover how Tom, a high school senior, uses four different presentations of the gospel to communicate with other high school students. In the first three, Tom shares with his good friend, Chris. In the last scenario, Tom shares his testimony with Jeff, whom he has just met. Read Tom's stories and note the style of each presentation. Think about which presentation seems most natural for you. Then follow the directions at the end of the chapter to be able to utilize the gospel presentation in your own life.

The beginning of the story . . .

Chris and Tom have been friends since grade school. They live in the same neighborhood, are in the same class at school, and both play on their school's football team.

Tom's Sunday School teacher recently encouraged the teens in his class to share Christ with their unsaved friends. Immediately Tom thought of Chris. Several times, Chris and his family had showed an interest in his church. To Tom this seemed like a good time to witness to Chris.

One chilly December afternoon, Tom and Chris stopped at

McDonald's after school. After several minutes of lively conversation about football and girls and college and girls and homework and girls, Tom asked Chris if it would be OK if they talked about something serious.

Option 1—One-Verse Evangelism

Pulling his New Testament from his backpack, Tom turned to Rom. 6:23 and asked Chris to read the verse. While Chris read, Tom wrote the verse on a paper napkin. Chris read:

"For the wages of sin is death, but the gift of God is eternal life in Christ Jesus our Lord."

Tom drew a box around the word *wages* in the verse like this:

FOR THE ⎡WAGES⎤ OF SIN IS DEATH,
BUT THE GIFT OF GOD IS ETERNAL
LIFE IN CHRIST JESUS OUR LORD.

Under the verse, Tom drew a cliff with the word *wages* inside like this:

WAGES

Tom asked Chris to share his understanding of the term *wages*. After listening to Chris's definition Tom said, "Wages are what a person earns. When a person sins, he is earning the wages of sin, and the wages of sin is death."

Tom then drew another box around the word *sin* in the verse and added the word *sin* to the diagram.

WAGES
SIN

Tom explained that according to the Bible, sin is more than doing wrong things; it is an attitude of disobedience toward God. He explained that everyone has violated God's commandments, even if it is only the first one, "Thou shalt have no other gods before me."

"That is why the Bible says, 'All have sinned,'" said Tom. Then, he drew another pair of lines to represent how sin separates us from God.

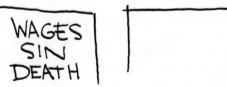

WAGES
SIN
DEATH

Tom explained to Chris how sin causes spiritual death and eternal separation from God. As he did this, Tom drew a box around the word *death* in the verse and added the word *death* to the diagram.

"Chris, the most important word in this verse is the little word *but*," Tom said. In his diagram, Tom wrote the word *but* between the two lines that represented separation.

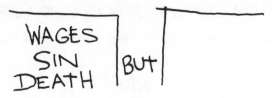

Tom extended his pen to Chris.

"If I offered this pen to you as a gift, what would you have to do to earn it?"

Chris reached for the pen and said, "If it is a gift, I don't do anything to earn it."

Tom continued, "Exactly, Chris. If it were a wage, you would have to do something. You would have to work for it. Since it is a gift, there are no strings attached. It is yours, free."

Tom drew another box around the word *gift* in the verse and wrote on the right side of his diagram like this:

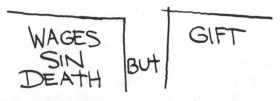

Tom then explained how God sent Jesus into the world to die for our sins. He told Chris how Jesus paid sin's penalty for every human being. Tom drew a box around the words *of God* in the verse and wrote them on the right side of his diagram:

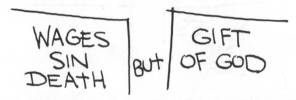

Tom explained to Chris how much God loves us, that only Jesus is qualified to save us, and how He lived and died without sin.

Tom then drew a box around the words *eternal life* in the verse and wrote them on the right side of his diagram:

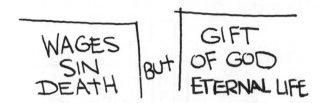

Tom explained that eternal life means just the opposite of death. "It not only means that we continue to live after we die but also means we are partners with God in His perfect plan right now."

At this point, Tom stopped. He asked Chris if there was anything he did not understand. Chris said, "No, everything seems pretty clear."

Tom drew a cross between the lines representing separation and wrote *Jesus* like this:

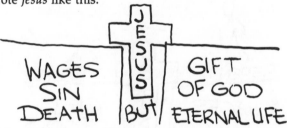

Tom went on, "Chris, Jesus suffered the penalty of death in our place. He died for us all so that none of us would be under the curse of death. The debt we could not pay, He paid for us.

"We must take two steps to receive the gift of God." Tom wrote the word *repent* above the left side of the diagram, like this:

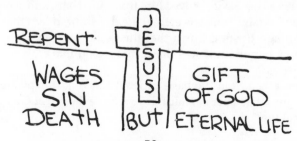
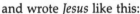

"To repent means to be willing to ask God's forgiveness for your sins and with His help, to turn away from the old way of life."

Turning back to his diagram, Tom wrote *believe* on the right side of the diagram.

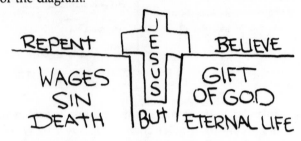

"Believing means trusting Jesus Christ for eternal life and salvation from your sins," said Tom. "Jesus is the only hope we have of eternal life. He is the bridge to life for us."

Tom drew a stick figure on the left side of the diagram, like this:

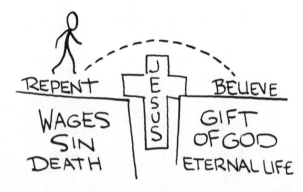

Tom wanted Chris to see how he must make a decision to move from one side to the other. He showed Chris how deciding to trust Jesus as his Savior moved him from sin, death, and separation to the gift of God, which is eternal life. He showed him that it was only through trusting Christ that this could happen. He emphasized how important it was that Chris would make his own personal decision.

Tom asked, "On the basis of what I have just explained, can you tell me what a person must do to receive the gift of God, which is eternal life?"

In his own words, Chris spoke of repenting, believing, and personally trusting Christ for salvation.

Tom knew the Holy Spirit was dealing with Chris. Tom said, "Chris, wouldn't you like to invite Jesus into your life, trusting Him right now for salvation and eternal life?"

Option 2—The Roman Road

Tom pulled his New Testament out of his backpack. Let's see, he thought, I think it's Rom. 3:23. He looked in the front of his Bible to double-check. Yep, there was the beginning reference just as he'd penciled in when he'd first learned of the Roman Road plan.

He showed the Bible to Chris and asked him to read the underlined verse.

"Notice this word," Tom said pointing.

"All?" Chris read.

"Yeah, all. That's a key word in this verse. You see everybody's sinned. I've sinned. Even you've sinned. To sin means to fall short of the mark. To be less than perfect. To fail God not only in our actions but even in our thoughts or our attitudes. To choose to go our way instead of God's. I don't know about you, but I don't have to look far in my life to see where I've messed up. Everybody's failed at some time or another, so everyone has sinned.

"Looks pretty hopeless, huh? Let's turn a few pages to Rom. 5:12." Tom glanced at Chris to see if he was still following or had lost interest—but it looked like Chris was right there with him.

"Let's check out this verse," he said pointing to Rom. 5:12.

"Want me to read it?" Chris asked.

"Sure," Tom replied.

Chris read slowly but more comfortably than he had been on the verse before. "Have you ever heard the story of Adam and Eve?" Tom asked.

"Sure. Or at least I know they ate an apple," Chris leveled.

"Well, because Adam and Eve chose to disobey God, sin entered into the world. Here, let's look at another verse." Tom quickly flipped to Rom. 6:23 and let Chris read it.

"OK," Tom continued, "what are wages?"

"What I get paid for working at Pizza Hut."

"Exactly," Tom concurred. "Only the wages talked about here aren't so pleasant. The result, or the payment, for our sin is death. So if we sin, then we deserve to die."

"Sounds pretty serious," Chris mumbled.

"It is, but it's not the end of the story, yet," Tom said, turning to Rom. 5:8. He read it and asked, "The payment for sin had to be made. Kinda' like one of our laws. When you break the law, you have to pay. And the payment for sin is eternity in hell when you die.

"But God wasn't any happier with that situation than we are. So He sent His only Son, Jesus, down to earth to live among us. Jesus never sinned. He's the only person who could say He didn't have to die because He hadn't sinned. But He loved us so much that He took our sins on himself just as if they were His sins. He died, not because of anything He'd done but because He loved us and wanted to take our punishment so we could live, so we could go to heaven when we die."

"So then if Christ died for us, so we don't have to go to hell, why do people make such a big fuss about religion?" Chris asked. "Aren't we all going to go to heaven then?"

"Good question," Tom replied, biting his lip. He turned to Rom. 10:8-13 and prayed for wisdom as he started trying to explain it in a way Chris would understand. The guys took turns reading—Tom reading one verse and Chris the next. "If I were going to give you a gift, when would it be yours?"

"When you gave it to me, of course."

"But what if you left the gift at my house and didn't take it home with you?" Tom insisted.

"Well, when you gave it to me, I'd take it, of course," Chris answered.

"Right." Tom breathed a sigh of relief. Chris seemed to still be following him. "It's kinda' that way with the gift of salvation. Jesus has died on the Cross so we can live—we can have this great gift of eternal life. But first we have to receive it by reaching out and taking it. By accepting that gift."

"What do you mean?" Chris asked.

"Like when someone confesses to a murder, what's he doing?"

"I guess he's admitting he did it."

"That's what it means here—if we admit we're a sinner, ask God to forgive us, and accept Jesus' death as the payment of our sins, we have eternal life."

"So that's what being a Christian is all about," Chris mused.

"Exactly. Here, let me show you one more verse." Tom turned

to Rom. 8:16 and read it. "When we accept Jesus into our hearts, we automatically become the sons of God."

"Can anybody be a son of God?" Chris asked. "Can anybody receive the gift?"

"Sure," Tom said with a smile. "Do you want to?"

"Yeah," Chris replied. "I think I do. Yeah. I do."

Option 3—Life Can Have True Meaning

"I've been thinking about something serious too," Chris mentioned between bites of Big Mac. "I thought that when we became seniors, suddenly everything in life would make sense," he mused. "Do you feel as hopeless as I do? Like there's no real purpose to life?"

"Well, not really," Tom replied. "I mean, being a senior is great, but I don't think I ever expected it to be the ultimate experience."

"So you're not dissatisfied with life?"

"There are sometimes little irritations, and worries, but overall, no, I'm not dissatisfied with life. For me, it's full of purpose and meaning."

"Yeah?"

"Yeah. Well, look, just a minute, let me show you something that might help explain it." Tom fumbled in his backpack until he found the pamphlet. "Here, this book pretty much sums it up for me."

Tom moved a sack of fries and put the booklet down where Chris could see it. Together they went through the first 11 pages, discussing the different things—some humorous—that one character had experimented with to try to find purpose in life.

Tom pointed to where it said, "Finally, I decided to check out the Bible," and said to Chris with a grin, "that's the same place I ended up . . . I figured I had nothing to lose."

"What'd you find there?"

"I know God loves me, and that He's in control of my life. For that matter, He loves you too—even if you do have ketchup all over your face," Tom chided with a grin. "In fact, God loves you so much that He sent His Son to die for you. Wanna hear more about it?"

Chris looked up from his french fries. "Yeah, go ahead."

Tom pulled his New Testament out of his backpack. He flipped it open to John 3:16 and read.

"You know, I think I've heard that before," Chris commented, as he reached for his shake.

"Probably. It's probably about the best-known verse in the Bible," Tom said. "But it's still full of great information."

Using the pamphlet and his Bible, Tom explained that God loved Chris and had a plan for his life—including a brand-new life for him, full of purpose and meaning.

However, he explained, sin keeps us from finding that life of purpose. Tom defined sin as man's walking his own way in rebellion against God, and that by walking away from God, we're walking away from a meaningful life. He pointed out that everyone has sinned and that the payment for sin is death.

Still looking up the scriptures that the pamphlet referred to, Tom told Chris that although we may try to find purpose in life, our own efforts can't save us. He revealed how Jesus died on the Cross in our place and rose again so that we can experience the ultimate, fulfilling life; a life of peace, freedom, and eternal life when we die.

"How do you get that life?" Chris asked, his forehead wrinkled.

"Well, you have to repent . . . to ask God for forgiveness," Tom answered.

"What in the world does repent mean?" Chris asked, slurping the last sip from his shake and starting in on a Coke.

"To repent means to be sorry for your sins," Tom explained. "We have to admit that we're sinners and that we have sinned. Then we have to be sorry for our sins, sorry enough to want our lives to be different. When we ask God to forgive our sins and receive Christ's gift of salvation, He promises to forgive us. In fact, He's waiting. There's nothing He'd rather do than forgive us. Here, let's look at the scriptures in Step 5."

The guys read through the pamphlet and as they got in the car, Tom said, "Chris, anytime you would be interested in praying that kind of prayer, I would love to be there with you."

"I'll think about it, Tom," Chris said.

Option 4—Evangelism Explosion

When Jeff heard about a special party after the football game, he decided to go. It was at a church, which kind of surprised Jeff— after all, he'd never heard of church kids going to football games together. But the party was fun. They had some goofy games and good food. Then, one of the guys in charge talked for a few minutes about how a person could have meaning and purpose in life only through a relationship with God. After he talked, he encouraged people to come to a special room if they didn't have a relationship with God but were interested in knowing more about it. Jeff mustered up his courage and went. There, he was paired up with one of the guys from his school, Tom.

After Tom introduced himself, Jeff was surprised how interested Tom seemed in his life. He asked questions about Jeff's favorite class at school and his family. They even talked for a minute about the football game. Before long, Jeff felt pretty comfortable with Tom—as if he'd known him for more than five minutes!

Next, Tom asked Jeff about his church. Jeff told him he'd gone to Sunday School as a kid, but not since then. Tom told Jeff about his church and about his personal relationship with God. He started talking about Christ and how he became a Christian. He told Jeff about the peace and fulfillment he'd found since he met Christ—he acknowledged that life wasn't always perfect, but now he had Someone to help him through the tough spots.

Then he turned it back around to Jeff, asking, "If you were to die tonight, do you know for certain that you'd go to heaven?"

"No, I don't," Jeff answered. "I guess that's one of the reasons I came back to talk to someone."

From that point, Tom shared the gospel with Jeff. First, he talked about eternal life and told Jeff that it was a free gift— something we can't earn by having good actions or attitudes.

Then Tom turned the focus to talk about the human race. He

explained how man has sinned, creating a gap between himself and God. He also reiterated that man cannot save himself.

Next, Tom started talking about God. He explained how much God loves us and wants us to spend eternity with Him in heaven. But he also explained about God's holiness, and how He must, as a just God, hold us accountable for our sins.

The following step was to explain to Jeff about Christ—that He's the Son of God and that He suffered for our sins, died and rose again so that we can have eternal life.

Finally, Tom explained how to receive Christ through faith and repenting of sins.

"Does this make sense to you?" Tom asked, looking closely for Jeff's reply.

"Yeah, it does," Jeff answered.

"Would you like to take this step and receive the gift of eternal life?"

"You know, I'd really like to do that," Jeff answered.

Tom told Jeff that praying is talking to God, just as they were talking together, and led him in a prayer.

"Let's look at one last verse," Tom said when they were through. He flipped his Bible to John 6:47 and asked Jeff to read it. "On the basis of what you just prayed, if you really meant it, you're now a child of God, a Christian. Not only that, but you're headed for an eternity in heaven!"

Outlines

The Roman Road

1. Turn to Rom. 3:23. Underline it and in the margin, write 5:12. The main idea of 3:23: All have sinned.

2. Turn to Rom. 5:12. Underline the verse and beside it write 6:23a. The main idea of 5:12: The penalty of sin.

3. Turn to Rom. 6:23a. Underline the verse and beside it write 5:8. The main idea of 6:23a: The penalty of sin.

4. Turn to Rom. 5:8. Underline the verse and write beside it 10:8-13. The main idea of Rom. 5:8: The provision of Jesus Christ.

5. Turn to Rom. 10:8-13. Underline the verses and write beside them 8:16. The main idea of Rom. 10:8-13: confession, repentance, and belief.

6. Turn to Rom. 8:16. Underline the verse. The main idea of Rom. 8:16: The assurance of the Spirit.

Life Can Have True Meaning

This version comes with a pamphlet for you to read through with your friend.

STEP 1: GOD LOVES YOU and Has a Plan for Your Life.

- His Love Includes You

  "For God so loved the world that he gave his one and only Son, that whoever believes in him shall not perish but have eternal life" (John 3:16).

- He Has New Life for You

  "I have come that they may have life, and have it to the full" (John 10:10).

STEP 2: SIN SEPARATES YOU from GOD and from OTHERS.

SIN is man's walking his own way in rebellion against God's will. When we walk away from God, we walk away from life.

- Everyone Has Sinned

  "For all have sinned and fall short of the glory of God" (Rom. 3:23).

- Sin Brings Death

  "For the wages of sin is death" (Rom. 6:23).

- Our Own Efforts Cannot Save Us

  "For it is by grace you have been saved, through faith—and this not from yourselves, it is the gift of God—not by works, so that no one can boast" (Eph. 2:8-9).

STEP 3: JESUS CHRIST DIED and ROSE AGAIN for our sins.

- He Died in Our Place

  "But God demonstrates his own love for us in this: While we were still sinners, Christ died for us" (Rom. 5:8).

- Jesus Christ Is the Way to New Life

  "Therefore, if anyone is in Christ, he is a new creation; the old has gone, the new has come!" (2 Cor. 5:17).

- He Gives Inner Peace

  "We have peace with God through our Lord Jesus Christ" (Rom. 5:1).

- And Freedom

  "So if the Son sets you free, you will be free indeed" (John 8:36).

- And Eternal Life

  "But the gift of God is eternal life in Christ Jesus our Lord" (Rom. 6:23).

STEP 4: YOU MUST REPENT and ASK GOD FOR FORGIVE-NESS.

- Admit and Confess Your Sins to God
  "He who conceals his sins does not prosper, but whoever confesses and renounces them finds mercy" (Prov. 28:13).
- Repentance Means:
  —to acknowledge your sins
  —to be sorry for your sins
  —to confess your sins
  —to be willing to forsake your sins
  —to have your life changed by Christ
- Forgiveness Is Promised
  "If we confess our sins, he is faithful and just and will forgive us our sins and purify us from all unrighteousness" (1 John 1:9).

STEP 5: PLACE YOUR TRUST IN CHRIST and RECEIVE HIM AS YOUR SAVIOR

- Christ Is Ready
  "Here I am! I stand at the door and knock. If anyone hears my voice and opens the door, I will come in" (Rev. 3:20).
- Receive Him Now
  "Yet to all who received him, to those who believed in his name, he gave the right to become children of God" (John 1:12).
- What to Pray
  Lord Jesus, I want to have life. I know that I have sinned. I need Your forgiveness and pardon. I believe that You died and rose again for my sins. I now accept You as my personal Savior. I will forsake my sinful life. I know that Your grace and power will enable me to live for You. Thank You, Jesus, for saving me and for giving me a new life.

Evangelism Explosion Outline

I. The Introduction
   A. Ask questions about his life
   B. Ask questions about his church background
   C. Share briefly about your own church
   D. Share your testimony—what your life was like before you met Christ, how you came to Christ, and the change in you after you became a Christian.

E. Two Questions
   1. Have you come to the place in your life where you know for certain that if you were to die today you would go to heaven?

      Transitional Question: Would you like for me to share with you how I made that discovery and how you can know it too?
   2. Suppose that you were to die tonight and stand before God and He were to say to you, "Why should I let you into My heaven?" What would you say?

II. The Gospel
   A. Grace
      1. Eternal life is a free gift (Rom. 6:23*b*).
      2. It is not earned or deserved (Eph. 2:8-9).
   B. Man
      1. Has sinned (Rom. 3:23).
      2. Cannot save himself (Eph. 2:9).
   C. God
      1. Is merciful; He wants you to go to heaven (2 Pet. 3:9).
      2. Is just; therefore He holds us accountable for our sins (Rom. 6:23*a*).
   D. Christ
      1. Who He is—the God-man (John 1:1, 14).
      2. What He did—
         a. Suffered and died for our sins (Isa. 53:6).
         b. Arose from the dead and is in heaven preparing a place for us (John 14:1-2).
         c. Offers us the gift of eternal life (1 John 5:11-12).
   E. Faith
      1. What it is not—merely knowing the "right answers" (James 2:19).
      2. What it is—repenting of our sins and trusting Christ alone for eternal life (Mark 1:15).

III. The Commitment
   A. The Clarifying Question: Does this make sense to you? (Rev. 3:20).
   B. The Commitment Question: Would you like to receive the gift of eternal life?
   C. The prayer of commitment.
   D. The assurance of eternal life (John 6:47).

To Think About, to Discuss, and to Do . . .

1. Look through the scriptures that have been presented in the chapter and decide which one(s) best explains salvation for you.

2. Do you know anyone like Tom? Is it possible for a teenager to be so confident in his testimony?

3. What will it take for you to be more like Tom?

4. Which of the four gospel presentations seems the most natural for you to try? Look back over the stories and the outlines and decide which one you want to memorize.

5. Work on memorizing the plan you choose and rehearse it several times with a Christian friend.

Beverly Burgess, the Evangelism coordinator at the Church of the Nazarene Headquarters; David Felter, the training director there; and Karen DeSollar and Jeanette Gardner of the youth department, all provided material for this chapter.

7

Doorways, Dangling Carrots, and Dining Room Tables

Reaching Your Friends for Jesus Through Special Events

Bud Reedy

So you are uncomfortable sharing with your friends about Christ. You get tongue-tied when they ask you about "this religion stuff." Well, don't lose heart, Bud Reedy is about to give you some handles on sharing your faith in a larger context—through special events. Reedy tells how the Lord can touch lives in surprising ways when believers gather together and how you can help be a part of those times. Be ready to think in bigger ways. What are some special events that you may be able to plug your friends into where they would be introduced to Jesus Christ?

You are about to enter a world of doorways, dangling carrots, and dining room tables. It's a world very much like the world you live in. The people you will meet are all connected with First Church, and they are probably just like you and your friends. They want to reach their teen friends for Jesus, but they are not quite sure where to start. Well, why wait? Let's get busy. Let's enter the lives and hearts of these people. Let's enter the world of doorways, dangling carrots, and dining room tables.

Scene One—"It's right under your nose"

Jimmy and Brent have been friends since the fifth grade. And they have a lot in common too. Like, for instance, the Seattle Sea-

hawks, Nike hightops, pizza (no mushrooms!), intramural sports, and an attraction for Cindy in fifth-period Algebra. They are a lot alike, these two guys.

But there is one major difference. Jimmy goes to First Church every Sunday, owns and pretty regularly reads his Bible, and belongs to Jesus. Brent, on the other hand, sleeps in on Sunday, doesn't know Barabbas from Beelzebub, and doesn't know Jesus. (He knows a little *about* Him, but he doesn't *know Him.*)

How can Jimmy begin to introduce his friend Brent to Jesus in a nonthreatening way, without feeling like he has to be superevangelistic and thump the family edition of the Bible over his head?

Scene Two—"Ah, thanks ... I think"

Rich has just been elected the new youth leader over at First Church. His pastor talks with him after the election.

"Congratulations, Rich," says Pastor Jones enthusiastically. "You're definitely the man for the job. You're young, you love Jesus,

you're likable, you love pizza. You're also the only one who would allow his name to appear on the ballot! You're our man all right!"

"Ah... thanks, Pastor ... I think. Anyway do you have any suggestions about how we can help our youth group grow? We've got a good corps of teens. The Sunday School class is going well, and the Wednesday night Bible discussion is attended fairly well by the group. But the group's not growing. Nobody's reaching out. I haven't seen a new teen come through our doors in months. What do you think we should do?"

What can Pastor Jones and Rich do to see the teen group start reaching out?

Scene Three—"Will she go, or will she turn me down?"

Julie is thinking about inviting her friend Amy to attend the

contemporary Christian concert First Church is promoting. It's being held over at the community college, and the whole teen group is going next Friday night. But Julie knows asking Amy to the concert will require some courage. Julie has a lot of questions dancing through her head:

"Will she go, or will she turn me down?"

"If she goes, will she have a good time?"

"Will the other teens in our group accept her?"

"Will this hurt our friendship?"

But Julie, because of her burden for Amy, prayed and fought through the fears and questions and asked her to go to the concert; and much to Julie's surprise, Amy attended and enjoyed it! Wow!

What should Julie do now that Amy has attended a church-sponsored youth activity?

Maybe you can identify with at least one of these scenarios. Whichever one you most identify with, whether you're a teen or a parent or a youth leader or a pastor, one thing is for sure: We are in this thing together. It is our responsibility to help reach unchurched teens for Jesus. So, let's explore how special events, special out-of-church activities may help Jimmy and Rich and Julie and *you* reach unchurched teens and grow a youth group.

Doorways—a response to scene one

Jimmy,

You've been thinking about how you could introduce your friend Brent to Jesus. And the answer has been right under your nose all along.

How about those church-sponsored youth activities? There's Sunday School, the Wednesday night Bible studies with Rich, and youth activities like:

the bowling party last week

the teen retreat in January

the gym night on Friday

the shopping spree this December

the film being shown next Sunday night

Up to this point, Jimmy, you've considered these activities merely as opportunities for your group to get together and have a good time (and by the way, there is nothing wrong with your group getting together and having a good time). But, what you've failed to see is that these special activities are doorways into the church—entry points for new teens like Brent to get into the flow of your youth group. Special events are a great way to introduce unchurched teens to Jesus.

Here's a few ways to best take advantage of doorways:

Step 1. *Realize you are the key!* How do you think the Christian faith spreads? Usually from one friend to another!

Not long ago, a group of 8,000 believers were asked what initially attracted them to Jesus.

2% said they were initially attracted to Jesus by TV/radio ministries

8% by the Bible

11% by their search for truth

47% said they were initially attracted to Jesus by a *person*

That's right, a person. And of the 47% who reported a person as their bridge to Jesus, 62% said that person was a friend or family member.

Jimmy, you are Brent's bridge to Jesus. And I'm glad God put Brent in your life. He did it for a reason, "that your light would so shine before Brent that he may see your good deeds and praise your Father in heaven" (Matt. 5:16, author's paraphrase).

When Benjamin Franklin wished to interest the people of Philadelphia in street lighting, he didn't try to persuade them by just talking about it. He hung a beautiful lantern on a long bracket in front of his home. He kept the glass brightly polished, and he carefully lit the wick every evening at the approach of dusk. People walking about on the dark streets saw Franklin's light a long way off and were drawn by its friendly glow. It wasn't long before Franklin's neighbors also began placing lights on brackets outside their homes. Soon the entire city realized the value of street lighting, and many followed his example with enthusiasm.

Don't miss the important spiritual lesson suggested by this story! As we let our lives glow with the love of Christ, we will influence others for Him. In fact, we may even encourage fellow believers to let their lights shine too.

Step 2. *Remember, prayer is where the battle starts.* Maybe you've never thought of it this way before, but there is a battle going on for Brent's heart. "Jimmy, your struggle is not against flesh and blood, but against the rulers, against the authorities, against the powers of this dark world and against the spiritual forces of the heavenly realms" (Eph. 6:12, author's paraphrase). Jimmy, it's war. And your most effective weapon is prayer.

Before you begin to develop a strategy for inviting Brent to a youth activity, pray for him.

Prayer is where the enthusiasm process begins. It is highly unlikely that Brent will come to Jesus unless you pray for him first. After all, isn't that how you came to Jesus? Didn't someone pray for you?

Step 3. *You need to invite him before he will attend.* The fact is that Brent is probably more open to the idea of your inviting him to a teen activity than you are. You are probably nervous about his response. Think positively. Brent likes sports and music and friends and pizza just as much as you do. Break the sound barrier the next time a youth activity is planned that you think Brent would enjoy attending. Invite him as your guest. You may be surprised at his response.

Step 4. *Remember, you cannot fail.* You heard right, Jimmy. You absolutely can't fail. Now, don't get me wrong. I do not mean that Brent will automatically accept your invitation, come to an activity, come to church, and invite Jesus into his life. I mean whether Brent accepts the invitation or not, you haven't failed. Why? Because God does not hold us responsible for the results. He asks only that we invite. He is responsible for the results.

God simply wants you to be available to Him when someone like Brent comes along. And God promises "success" if you faithfully invite your friends. "Jimmy, serve wholeheartedly, as if you were serving the Lord, not men, because you know that the Lord will reward you for whatever good you do" (Eph. 6:7-8, author's paraphrase).

In other words, Jimmy, the only way you could fail Brent is if you fail to invite him. Invite Brent to your youth group's next activity. You cannot fail!

Dangling Carrots—a response to scene two

Rich,

Your election to the position of youth leader at First Church could very well be the beginning of one of the most demanding yet rewarding periods of your life. Working with teens is challenging.

It will require your best effort. You are the key to seeing your teen group grow, both spiritually and numerically.

It is your responsibility to schedule meaningful, exciting, fun, *outreach-oriented* (growth) activities for your group. You must set the tone for reaching out to others. Take the following steps to start the process.

1. *Schedule a meeting of the youth ministry resource people in your local church.* Invite Pastor Jones. Meet with the other youth leaders as soon after your election to leadership as possible. Then, as a group, pray. Evaluate. Plan. Program. Pray again. Make group decisions.

2. *Discuss growth goals for the group.* Ask: "Where do we want our group to go?" Setting growth goals is one way to assure that your youth program is headed in the right direction. Make sure your teens are given the opportunity to help establish the growth goals so that they will use them. Once you've established some growth goals, write out specific objectives for the year.

3. *Evaluate the existing programs and activities.* Talk about what is meeting the needs of your young people and what may not be meeting needs. Be honest. Ask: "Will our present program and activities help us reach our growth goals?" Reinforce the activities that will help your group grow and reconsider those activities that retard growth. It will be tough, but it is necessary if your group is to grow.

4. *Consider the church's overall mission when discussing youth ministry growth goals.* That's why it is so important to have Pastor Jones there. Your growth goals should reflect, even coincide with, the church's goals for ministry in the community.

5. *Plan for the implementation of these growth goals.* Planning is: deciding in advance
> *what* should be done
> *why* it should be done
> *where* it should be done
> *when* it should be done
> *how* it should be done

Now, let's talk about planning activities to reach unchurched teens. You've got teens in your group that, if encouraged, would invite their friends to the right activities. Like Jimmy. He would invite his friend Brent to a church-sponsored teen activity if *you* would challenge him to. Jimmy is Brent's doorway into your group, but you must provide the *dangling carrot,* the program or activity that will entice Brent. Here are a "bunch" of dangling carrots to choose from, activities that could be scheduled in response to your growth goals.

Dangling Carrot 1—Youth Rallies

A rally is a gathering of your youth group for the purpose of fellowship, bridge-building, and evangelism. Using team competition, games are played that are competitive and fun. Give prizes to the winning teams. Then a message is shared and refreshments served.

Sound like a simple concept? Well, it is! But do not let the simplicity of the activity fool you. Youth rallies are a tried-and-proven growth activity. Team competition is a fun way to involve the whole group, build community, and make new people (like Brent) feel comfortable. It provides motivation for attending future events too.

Interested? Well, if you think you might like to try a youth rally, here are a few simple things you can do to prepare:
—select a location (fellowship hall, local gym, etc.)
—advertise (newsletter, bulletin, word-of-mouth announcements, etc.)
—encourage teens to invite their unchurched friends (your teens are the doorways)
—determine the number of teams you wish to have (6 to 10 teens per team is best)
—appoint an adult to lead each team
—secure prizes for the winning team
—pray for your teens as they invite their unchurched friends to the rally

Dangling Carrot 2—Youth Retreats

Does your youth group have an annual retreat? If not, this can be a very effective way to reach some of your growth goals. In a Gallup survey, over 50 percent of teens said that they would attend a spiritual life retreat, if invited by a friend.

A retreat can be a great source of fun, excitement, fellowship, recreation, Bible discovery, sharing, evangelism, growth, and life change. Every participant should bring at least one unchurched friend along on the retreat.

As with all activities, there are some things you can do to make the retreat a success. Don't miss the basic details.

Like setting goals and objectives. What is it, specifically, that you wish to accomplish during this retreat?

Like promoting. Promotion is so important, you may consider recruiting an adult or teen whose sole responsibility is promoting the retreat. Your plans may be fantastic, your speaker the best around, and your location second to none, but unless you can get the word out, teens will not attend.

Like recruiting the right workers. Having the right speaker, adult leaders, and sponsors at your retreat is of extreme importance. Adult sponsors should be chosen right from the adults of your church.

Like programming and scheduling. The options for retreat programming and scheduling are limited only by your imagination. When considering the program, establish a theme for the retreat. Themes can include: finding God's will, discipleship, being a believer in a non-Christian world, temptation, the Lordship of Jesus, or peer pressure. Select a theme based on the needs of your group and the goals of the retreat. Once a theme is selected, use it on all publicity. Contact your speaker and make him aware of it so that he can design his messages accordingly. And most importantly, design your activities, as best you can, around the theme.

Like the right location. The site for the retreat is rather important. Begin by asking your pastor or other youth directors about retreat locations in your area. An organization called Christian Camping International, P.O. Box 646, Wheaton, IL 60187, produces a book titled *Official Guide to Christian Camps and Conference Centers*.

Like scheduling. A typical retreat schedule needs to be active enough to keep energy high and everybody excited, but not so crowded that there is no time to form friendships, spend time in reflection, and enjoy a place away from the day-to-day grind. The thing to remember about scheduling is the need for adaptability and flexibility.

Dangling Carrot 3—Revivals

Most likely, your local church schedules at least one, possibly two revivals a year. Right? Usually lasting about a week, these revival services feature a special speaker and music. The whole purpose of revival services is to "wake up" your church; to return your church to a state of deep commitment to the Lord Jesus Christ.

Many churches have taken specific steps to involve their teens in the services, and some churches have discovered revival services can be another successful entry point for new teens into the church. Revivals can help your group reach its growth goals. Here are some suggestions you may consider to involve your teens and their unchurched friends in the revival services at your church.

1. *Discover the purpose.* Sit down with your pastor and discuss his plans for the revival services. Ask him what the purpose of the revival is and what he envisions for the church through revival.

2. *Plan a youth emphasis.* Discuss the possibility of a youth night. A Friday or Saturday night is best.

3. *Plan with teens in mind.* Plan activities for that evening that will be appealing to teens and are designed to involve teens, such as:

- —a contemporary Christian singing group
- —a teen choir
- —special songs by teens
- —teen ushers, greeters, song leaders, scripture readers, etc.
- —a youth-oriented message by the evangelist
- —an afterglow following the service featuring pizza or some other popular snack that will encourage teens to attend

4. *Invite.* Encourage your teens to bring unchurched friends with them.

Dangling Carrot 4—Sunday School

"Sunday School? Are you kidding? You mean that Sunday School can help our teen group meet its growth goals?"

Yes, that's precisely what I mean. The Sunday School has been and continues to be a unique and indispensable part of a well-balanced youth program. It's the natural and possibly the best place to teach Christian doctrine and the Bible to teens. No doubt,

Sunday School played a big part in your growth and development as a young Christian. Well, the teens in your group deserve the same opportunity to grow in Christlikeness. Sunday School is a great setting for discipleship and small-group interaction.

And the Sunday School can also become an active entry point for new teens into the church. After attending an all-church or all-teen group function, the Sunday School is a great place to help that new teen become better acquainted with a small group his own age. The Sunday School would be a great place for Jimmy to invite Brent and Julie to invite Amy after Friday night's teen group activities.

Dangling Carrot 5—Special Outings

We've talked about youth revivals and retreats, teen Sunday School, and youth rallies. We've covered all the bases, right?

Wrong! There is another world out there beyond the four walls of your church to be explored, another strategy to be developed that may help you reach your growth goals: Friday night and Saturday outings!

There are places to go, things to see, activities to do, all of which can make excellent entry points for new teens into your group. Fun, nonthreatening group activities that Jimmy, Julie, and the rest of the teen group will enjoy doing and invite their unchurched friends to (like Brent and Amy).

Activities can include: hikes, shopping sprees, bowling, professional sporting events, hayrides, contemporary Christian concerts, camping, recreation nights, putt-putt golf, roller skating, swimming, etc. The list goes on and on, limited only by your imagination and the interest of your teens.

To utilize such activities as opportunities for your group to grow, careful planning of these special outings is important.

Rich, you're beginning to see how important your job is, aren't you? And it's coming into sharper focus now what your job is: to provide the dangling carrots, the programs, and to encourage your teens to attend those programs and invite their friends. Don't be discouraged. Keep praying. Keep challenging your teens to invite their individual friends. For the day will come when Jimmy's friend Brent or Julie's friend Amy or another of your teen friends will show up at an activity. They will have a good time, and come again, and find Jesus. And then you'll know it was worth it!

Dining Room Tables—a response to scene three

Congratulations, Julie. You did it. You invited your friend Amy to a teen activity and she came! Wow! Amy hasn't met Jesus yet, but it's a real big step in the right direction.

And weren't you just a little surprised by Amy's response? The fact is, she was more receptive than you thought she would be.

That's because:

Amy is fairly new at school.

She needed friends (like you).

She is experiencing a lot of change in her life.

She has a lot in common with you and the rest of your group.

Pastor Jones, Rich, and you were praying.

The Holy Spirit is drawing her to Jesus.

Now, Julie, it is very important that *you* follow up on Amy and show her some special attention. You are the key, not Pastor Jones, not Rich, but you. Rich provided the dangling carrot, but you are her doorway into the church.

Julie, if you go to Amy's house to visit her within 36 hours of the concert, if you sit around her dining room table and visit and invite her to the next First Church activity, there is an 85% chance she will go with you. (If Pastor Jones or Rich visits her, there is only a 43% chance she will return.)

I'm serious, Julie. You're Amy's doorway to Jesus.

And if she does come to another activity, visit with her again. But this time, make it *your* dining room table. Invite her over for dinner. Your open heart is the key. Cultivate your friendship, your common interests. Make another date to play tennis or bowl or watch a video.

And who knows. One day you may have the once-in-a-lifetime experience of introducing Amy to Jesus. Wouldn't that be something?

To Think About, to Discuss, and to Do . . .

1. Read Acts 10:1-8, 23b-27. How did Cornelius implement this idea of special event evangelism to reach out to his family and friends?

2. How would you explain to a friend at church the ideas of "Doorways," "Dangling Carrots," and "Dining Room Tables"? Which one is most important in reaching others for Christ?

3. Who do you most identify with, Jimmy, Rich, or Amy? What steps can you take to overcome any fears or frustrations you may have concerning special event evangelism?

4. Are there any special events coming up in your church or community within the next two weeks? Who can you invite? Call the person and invite him to go with you.

5. Plan a special event. Talk to your pastor and friends about the need of a special event that will help your youth group introduce others to the church and ultimately to Jesus Christ. Get a committee together to plan and implement the event.

Bud Reedy is pastor of First Church of the Nazarene, York, Pa. He has written and edited youth resources and founded a community outreach center for teens in Oxford, Pa.

8

That's What Friends Are For

Helping Others with Their Spiritual Needs

David Busic

If we sincerely want to share our faith and if we are obedient when God presents those opportunities, sooner or later someone will need spiritual guidance. Our pastor or youth leader won't always be around, so we need to know how to offer some help ourselves. This chapter will explain some principles of spiritual guidance. It will also offer some specific ideas you can use when counseling someone about these matters. Will you know how to respond when someone comes to you with a spiritual problem?

The need for sound spiritual guidance

I'll never forget one of my early experiences seeking spiritual help. I was 13 years old and was in a Sunday worship service. The pastor had just given an invitation to come to the altar at the front of the church and pray. I slipped out of my seat and began that long walk down the aisle to the front of the church. I'll admit I was a bit afraid of what my family and friends might think, but I was trying to be sensitive to the Lord's leading. This anxiety was soon replaced by a greater problem when I reached the altar.

My knees had no sooner met the carpet and my head touched the altar than I was surrounded on every side. (I understood how

Custer felt at the Little Big Horn.) I lifted my elbow from the altar and peeked underneath to see who had come to pray with me. There were several of the saints of the church who had come to "pray me through." Brother Jones began to lead out in prayer, and soon the others joined in. Someone to my left began to shout, "Let go!" and someone on my right hollered, "Hang on!" Sister Smith was playing the seventh stanza of "Just as I Am" on the organ, and her foot was getting a little heavy on the amplifying pedal. Sensing some competition for volume, Brother Jones began to pump up the decibels of his prayer.

Suddenly, someone was patting, or rather, pounding me on the back, and somebody else began to force-feed me Kleenex. My head had started to swim from all the voices: "Pray through!" "Give it to God!" "Lay it all on the altar!" I could hardly concentrate on my prayer for all the noise. I had almost given up hope when I felt someone gently touch my arm, and I heard a familiar voice above the din. "David, is there something I can help you pray about?" It was my junior high Sunday School teacher. With a sigh of relief, I lifted my head, and with moist eyes and a somewhat confused look on my face, said, "I came to pray about my friend."

I learned a valuable lesson that day. I discovered the essential need for trained and sensitive spiritual counselors in a variety of settings. It was not that Brother Jones and the others were not supportive and concerned. They had come to pray with me precisely *because of* their love and concern. The problem was simply that they had never learned how to deal with someone seeking spiritual help.

Me? A spiritual guide?

Many Christians are afraid to pray or talk with someone who has expressed a spiritual need. Most people feel inadequate to offer spiritual guidance. We tend to leave that up to the experts; that is, the professional clergy. But people need spiritual help in situations other than church settings around the altar when the pastor is readily available. Camp and retreat settings, a ride in a car, or even an informal talk in a restaurant or at home may all present an opportunity for you to be a spiritual guide.

The two most commonly expressed fears are "What would I say?" and "Why would they want to hear from me?" These questions miss the point of spiritual guidance. The issue is not our ability or adequacy but is rather God's desire and ability to work through us to help others. We *can* and *should* be a channel of God's grace to others who are in need of spiritual help.

What to DO as a spiritual guide

How do we respond when a friend has a spiritual need? What should we do, and not do, as we attempt to encourage, counsel, give support, and pray for him? Our responses will be different, in varying degrees, as we are sensitive to each individual person. However, there are several principles of spiritual guidance that will remain the same in every situation.

1. *DO ask for the Holy Spirit's guidance.* It is true that we are not capable of handling spiritual matters alone. God, however, has promised that when *you* do not have the words and wisdom, He does. The Gospel of John has a lot to say about the Holy Spirit's guidance in our lives. John 14:26 says that the Holy Spirit "will teach you all things and will remind you of everything I [Jesus] have said to you." All you have to do is ask. Seeking God's direction when helping with spiritual guidance should be continuous.

2. *DO speak personally.* Spiritual guidance is most significant if you have a relationship with the person. Friends and peers are the best sources of spiritual help. When you pray or talk with someone about spiritual matters, it is usually best that guys help guys and girls help girls. Speaking about one's spiritual life is an intimate thing to do, in any situation. Since people feel safe talking with someone of their own gender, it's wise to do all we can to make them feel comfortable when sharing their needs and problems.

It is also best that you face the person with whom you are speaking. This will enable you to be more convenient to talk with, and to be more accessible for direct eye-to-eye contact.

If you are in a large-group setting and you do not know the person, it is important to be personal by introducing yourself. "My name is (your name). What is your name?" By using the person's first name, you identify yourself as a friend, helping that person feel at ease to open up to you.

3. *DO help clarify the need.* Perhaps the most complicated part of spiritual guidance is identifying the person's need. One of the first questions you may ask is, "What can I do to help you?" or "Is there something I can help you pray about?" Their response to your initial question may be vague: "I just can't go on anymore" or "I want what the preacher was talking about" or "I'm not sure." It is part of your responsibility to help the person clarify the need.

A good question to bring that need into perspective is "What do you think God wants you to do?" Urge him to be specific, for it is important to get a definite answer. Ask him as many questions as necessary to bring his need into focus. However, remember that your job is not to psychoanalyze him and tell him his need. It is to help *him* pinpoint his need so that God can begin to deal with that issue in his life.

4. *DO use scripture.* Once you have assisted someone in identifying his need, you can begin to give spiritual direction. God has given you a mind, and He wants you to use your common sense. However, your human wisdom is not enough; you will also need your Bible.

I recently polled a local teen group. My question to them was, "How many of you have had someone who was praying and sharing scripture with you?" Only two of the entire group said they had. We do not counsel to share our personal biases and convictions. Our human advice cannot establish or build faith in God. Only God's Word can do that.

It is most helpful to have your Bible with you in a spiritual counseling situation. It guides you in your speech and helps the other person see and understand what you are saying. If you write down some verse references, it will be invaluable to him in the days that will follow.

Because you cannot anticipate every opportunity for offering spiritual help, you may not always have your Bible with you. Therefore, you should memorize a few key verses of Scripture. If the situation calls for forgiveness, 1 John 1:9 or Rev. 3:20 are good verses to use. If the person wants to be filled with the Holy Spirit, 1 Thess. 5:23-24, Acts 15:8-9, and Eph. 3:14-19 are excellent sources. An appropriate verse for nearly any altar situation is 1 John 1:7, which speaks about "walking in the light" God has given us.

5. *DO share personal experiences.* While God's Word should always be a priority in your counseling, your personal experience will be of value as well. Once you understand the need in the other person's life, share how God has worked in your life in a similar situation. It need not be an identical problem, but the truth that God is able to help us and will not leave us will speak to any issue. Describe how you were feeling at that time and how God gave you the strength and understanding to deal with the situation. Remember, your task is to emphasize God and not yourself.

6. *DO pray together.* End your counseling time by praying a vocal prayer. Now that you are aware of the specific need, you can pray specifically. The closing prayer is a form of faith and affirmation for the other person. After the prayer, remind him of the key verse of Scripture you have shared, and offer your continued support.

7. *DO follow up.* It is very important that you attempt to make personal contact with your counselee following your counseling time, especially if he prayed to receive Christ. The days following any new spiritual commitment are decisive, and all the support, love, and encouragement that can be given are invaluable in establishing someone's faith.

The first contact should be made the day following your conversation about spiritual matters. You may use either a telephone call or a personal visit. The conversation does not need to be lengthy. Just long enough to remind the person of your prayers and God's ability to do what His Word has promised. Later in the week, a short handwritten note would also give much-needed encouragement. Your personal follow-up gives a tangible expression of your genuine concern for the other person and his relationship with God.

What NOT to do as a spiritual guide

In addition to what you should do in a counseling situation at the altar, or another location, there are some no-no's.

1. *DON'T dominate the conversation.* One of the keys to any

interpersonal communication is to be a good listener. Those who talk more than they listen usually miss the subtle yet critical details of a conversation. Being a good listener is not simply hearing words, though. It also involves reading between the lines and being aware of the speaker's body language as well. Some people speak more clearly through their actions than by their words.

Listening for every detail creates a sensitivity within you to be able to detect not only the other person's need but the Holy Spirit's direction as well.

2. DON'T generalize the need. We have briefly mentioned the importance of identifying a specific need. Those who help others with spiritual guidance sometimes offer all-encompassing explanations and prayers, which only confuse the situation.

You must determine the need and then be specific. If someone's problem is sin in his life, urge him to confess and seek forgiveness. If he is struggling with the future and what direction to take, share promises for God's guidance. If he is worried about a friendship, point him to a scripture about God's design for Christian relationships. Whatever the need, give attention to the specific nature of that concern.

3. DON'T use religious language. By religious language I am not speaking of the essentials of the Christian faith. There are certain words we do not and cannot afford to lose. What I am talking about is "church jargon." We ministers are especially guilty of this. For instance, "Take hold of the horns of the altar, until you get the glory down, and ride the heavenly train to Zion!" There is nothing wrong with the thought behind that statement. However, when we speak in clichés, we assume that people understand our cultural background and our religious tradition, which is not always the case. You must be able to present the gospel and pray with others in terms *they* can understand.

4. DON'T overemphasize feelings. Because our emotional and spiritual lives are closely related, people often confuse the two. We may think that spiritual growth must be accompanied by great emotional displays. However, a person does not have to have an emotional experience to satisfy a spiritual need. Feeling is great if and when it comes, but our salvation and spiritual growth are not rooted in feelings.

A good balance to an emphasis on feelings is to stress assurance. Assurance is the faith to believe that what God has promised in His Word is true and that what He has promised He will do. That affirmation is much deeper than an emotional response. You have a certain responsibility as a spiritual guide to lead others to an assurance of God's action in their lives.

5. *DON'T talk someone out of what he already has.* You must be careful that you do not discount someone's past spiritual experiences. If he can look back to a time when he was forgiven of his sins, and has no unconfessed sin in his life, then he does not need to pray the "sinner's prayer" again. Highlight his current relationship with Christ.

You may be counseling someone who is doing his best to be a Christian but is having difficulty being consistent. This may indicate a need for entire sanctification, or it may simply reflect a need for greater personal discipline. In any situation you should not press someone into an experience for which he is not yet ready spiritually. It is very important that you make that person aware of God's desire and ability to deal with him on whatever spiritual level he may be.

Doubt is common among those who seek spiritual help. Help them see that God has already accomplished for them all that they need to be Christian. Scripture is the key to overcome doubt.

6. *DON'T ignore the community of faith.* You may have many opportunities to share and help someone spiritually in a one-on-one conversation. However, there are times when spiritual help can be given in a group context such as during an altar call or in a group discussion on a retreat. Anyone who needs spiritual guidance should know that he is part of a community (church family).

If you are leading the conversation in a group setting, it is important to note the presence of these fellow Christians and supporters. There may be times when you will not be available to help again, while another member of your group could. And the more encouragement and support a person receives, the more likely he is to grow spiritually.

Additionally, there may even be more than one in the group struggling with the same issue, and they need to find an answer to their own spiritual problem. The words you speak and the scriptures you share may be just what meets the needs of several different people.

You can do it!

It is never easy to guide someone into a strong relationship with Jesus Christ. You may think that you are not qualified to help someone else with his spiritual growth. But just as we have an obligation to lead others to Christ, so too are we obligated to walk with them all along their journey of Christian discipleship. If you are sensitive to God's leading and are informed as you counsel and pray with others, God will enable you to be a spiritual guide.

To Think About, to Discuss, and to Do . . .

1. Read Col. 4:2-6. What are Paul's instructions for answering non-Christians' spiritual questions? What does he say about helping fellow Christians? (See Eph. 4:29.) What is different about these situations? What is similar?

2. No one wants to appear spiritually conceited or holier-than-thou. Why should we not let this hinder us from helping someone as their spiritual counselor?

3. Try to remember a time when you needed some spiritual advice or help. Did someone help you? How did he help? Now try to recall an opportunity you had to help someone else spiritually. Did you help? Why or why not?

4. Think of someone you know who needs some spiritual guidance. Pray for that person right now. Pray that God would show you if and when you should counsel and/or pray with that person.

5. Try to improve your communication skills. Read some books or articles that deal with interpersonal communication.

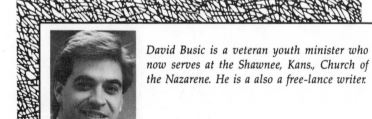

David Busic is a veteran youth minister who now serves at the Shawnee, Kans., Church of the Nazarene. He is a also a free-lance writer.

9

Follow-up

How to Help a New Christian Stay Alive and Thrive

Mark Gilroy

> *"I had a friend who got saved at camp, but within a week, he sure didn't act like a Christian anymore." All of us have seen young Christians who lose their spiritual life. Mark Gilroy writes about the part we play in helping our friends stay alive as new Christians. As you read, think about the person who has most encouraged you as a young Christian, and a person you need to help stay alive and thrive.*

It can be a cold world out there

Margaret Leonard opened her front door at 7:15 A.M., just like she did every weekday as she headed for the bus stop and on to her office. This particular winter's morning she stopped short and sharply drew in her breath. It wasn't the bitter 11-degree fahrenheit air that made her gasp. There on her welcome mat was a small bundle that looked like, but couldn't be, but was, a small baby.

She gathered the chilled infant close to her and hurried in from the frigid cold. She wasn't a nurse or a doctor, but she understood enough to know that the bluish skin meant the baby was near death or had already crossed that threshold. She put her face next to the baby's. No breath. Margaret began mouth to mouth resuscitation as best she knew how, while her fingers fumbled to punch out 911.

The little bundle was so still. She gently massaged to warm the baby and restore circulation. She blew light breaths into still lips. She marveled at such tiny fingers, hoping desperately that they would clutch at her finger. The closed eyelids were almost translucent. She wondered if the ambulance and paramedics would ever arrive.

They did. In record time. Just under 10 minutes. They took over for the frantic Margaret but ceased efforts shortly after. The baby—it was a boy—was dead. The coroner estimated that he had died less than an hour earlier.

Two days later, after intense investigation, police found and arrested his mother. She confessed almost immediately. Without a job or family, she felt that she couldn't handle a baby and had decided to leave him with someone else. She used to work with Margaret and knew that she would be a wonderful mother. She never meant for things to turn out this way. She had only left the baby out for two hours. She just hadn't realized how cold it was outside. She thought the blankets were warm enough. He would be OK.

Poor little six-pound, five-ounce, dark-haired baby boy, born into a cold, cold world. He never heard his name called. What could his mother have been thinking? How could she abandon such a precious little bundle of life?

You've probably read stories like this one before. And you know it happens all the time. But did you know that it's not just babies who die this way?

It can get real cold when you're on your own

Cindy felt a void in her life. Homelife wasn't real bad, but then it wasn't real great either. Sure, she understood that her family was well off, but she also understood that they paid for it. Her dad worked almost all the time, either traveling, at his office, or at home. Cindy and her mother were used to getting along without him, even when he was present. She and her mom didn't talk that much anymore anyway.

A friend from school, Dana, invited Cindy to a retreat at her church. Cindy hadn't gone to church very often and didn't know much about religious things—her mom was Jewish and her dad Catholic, so as a compromise they hadn't practiced any religion. She had certainly never been to anything like a retreat. It was hard to understand and seemed almost foreign, especially all the talks they had. Every three or four hours they all gathered in the central room where a special speaker addressed them. Interesting, but different.

Even though the whole experience was so alien to anything she was used to, Cindy liked it. She couldn't remember the last time she had laughed so much. Everybody was so friendly and so close. It was never this way at school, not even with her best friends. People talked about their problems, and cried, and prayed. It was like the family she had always wanted.

What the speaker had to say during the last "talk" made a lot of sense to her. He spoke about being a new person through Jesus Christ. He shared how to receive this new life. He invited the entire group to pray a simple prayer with him. Cindy did. And when he asked those who had prayed the prayer to raise their hands, Cindy did.

But she didn't really know what had happened to her; it was confusing. And no one was really available to explain it to her. She was going to go to the Wednesday night teen meeting that first week after retreat, but her mom had already made plans for the two of them to shop. She would have gone to church Sunday, but it was hard to ask her parents for a ride on the one morning they slept in; they definitely wouldn't understand. Dana lived too far away to come pick her up, and Cindy hadn't talked to her for several days anyway. In fact, she hadn't talked that week to anyone from the retreat. They had seemed so friendly.

She did show up on the following Wednesday, and on a Sunday morning several weeks later. But, it wasn't like retreat. There wasn't the same family feeling. People weren't as interested in her now. For about a month Cindy feebly held on to the faith she had found in that simple little prayer; but then, quietly, Cindy died. Not physically. Spiritually. It's a cold, cold world when you have to make it alone.

Your response will make the difference

Count on it. Sometime, someplace, you are going to hold a newborn person in your arms. Not a baby with tiny little fingers and toes, but a newborn Christian. Maybe at a retreat, maybe during a morning worship service, maybe in your family room, someone will respond to the good news that their sins can be forgiven and their lives changed by Jesus Christ. And what you do, how you respond to that newborn, will help determine whether he lives or dies, grows or perishes, as a Christian. Notice I didn't say, what the *church* does, or what the *pastor* says, or how your *youth leader* responds. I said, it is how *you* respond that will in large part make the difference.

We don't expect new babies to survive without tender loving care. We shouldn't expect new Christians to either. Our job is to act like the workers in the church nursery. You can help new Christians eat, crawl, walk, and with God's grace, run. You are called to encourage others to grow! Some of your friends will either live or die, depending upon on how you respond to the challenge.

Here are a few simple steps to help you help someone else stay alive and thrive.

How to help keep a new Christian alive and thriving...

1. *Seek God's help.* Just as we cannot be saved through human effort, so too, any ministry we will ever hope to have is dependent upon God's grace. You can't save yourself or anyone else, and you can't make anybody keep being a Christian no matter how hard you work.

What you can do is be a willing instrument of God. You can pray for sensitivity and the ability to encourage. You can humbly acknowledge that you must depend on God for success.

2. *Realize that your efforts do matter.* No, you can't save anybody and you can't make anybody keep being a Christian, but you do have a real and vital role in the process. In Eph. 2:8-9, Paul emphasizes that salvation is through grace, not works. We can't earn it, it's a gift. In the very next verse, though, Paul says, "We are God's workmanship, created in Christ Jesus to do good works, which God prepared in advance for us to do."

Salvation is a gift that you can't receive for someone else. But, you can make a difference in his life. Even with your weaknesses. Even with your idiosyncrasies. You can be the difference between life and death. Accept the challenge and get involved.

3. *Provide time and friendship.* New Christians need most of all someone who cares for them. They need friendship and encouragement. They need someone who will listen. They need someone they can watch. In other words, new Christians need someone who will give them time. And the younger a Christian they are, the more time they require.

It is vital that you establish contact with a new Christian within 24 hours, and again within 72 hours of his conversion. This is when most new Christians wonder if anything actually happened to them; they easily get discouraged and give up. After those first few days, you should plan to meet with a new Christian at least once a week. You may talk specifically about Christian matters or just spend some time together. In addition, send cards and make phone calls; these are simple yet powerful ways of saying, "I care."

Just remember, when people feel loved and supported by a group, it seems natural to embrace that group's beliefs. That is likely why Cindy got saved on the retreat. But, when people don't feel loved and supported by a group, it becomes very confusing and difficult to embrace the group's beliefs. Is it any wonder that Cindy quit believing and died spiritually?

4. *Help the person learn the basics of the faith.* Do you ever feel like you spend too much time at church; that you're there all the time? You've heard everything before; at least six times? Maybe you grew up in the church. If this is the case, you are one of the rare and fortunate ones!

Fewer and fewer people are growing up in traditional families where church attendance is part of their upbringing. A survey in *Seventeen* magazine revealed that less than 25 percent of teenagers now live in homes where there is regular church attendance.

This means that many people have very little religious knowledge or experience to draw on when they get saved. Some say that much of North America and Europe is now a post-Christian society and that paganism has reasserted itself. As a result, many are illiterate when it comes to spiritual issues. They know nothing of the Bible, the Christian faith, right and wrong.

Even many who grow up in the church may have no concept of Christianity. By the time you graduate from high school you will have spent over 12,000 hours in school. If you are an average TV viewer, you will have spent 16,000 hours in front of the TV. But even if you attend every Sunday School class, every worship service, including Sunday night, and every weeknight service from birth to the end of your senior year of high school, you will have received less than 4,000 hours of formal religious training. And that's only if you paid attention!

The point is, new Christians need to be grounded in the faith. They need to learn the importance of God's Word. They need to be shown the way to work out their salvation with fear and trembling.

A little later, I will mention one simple resource you can use to help you with this. But no one resource will be enough. If you are to help new Christians survive and thrive, part of your challenge will be to recommit yourself to knowing what it means to be a Christian.

Don't forget what was said in number 3, though. Your friends who are new Christians must learn and grow primarily through your time and friendship. Christianity is more "caught" than "taught."

5. *Involve the person with other Christians.* Even if a new Christian is your best friend, and you are the one who introduced him to Jesus Christ, he will need to build relationships with other Christians. Do all you can to involve him in the life of your church and youth group. He will need to see and hear from a variety of Christians as he learns what it means to be a follower of Jesus Christ.

Introduce him to friends, youth leaders, and your pastor. If he is asking questions you can't answer, or has problems you can't help solve, help him meet the people in your church who can help.

6. *Have a plan.* You know that you need God's help. Check.
You know that you can make a difference. Check.
You must provide time and friendship. Check.
You must help involve him with other Christians. Check.
Hey, we skipped number 4.

You must introduce him to the basics of the Christian faith. Uh. Well. Hmmm . . . Maybe you could use some help. There is a great little resource that provides that help. It's a small envelope of materials called *Now That I'm a Christian: Basic Bible Studies for Youth*. It was designed to help you keep new Christians alive and thriving. It deals with the basics of the faith, and it's a great place to start. You can use the eight simple Bible studies, two tracts, and a certificate to lead a friend through the basics of the faith. Is it really that easy? Yes. You simply need to go through all the lessons once yourself to familiarize yourself with what is there.

Now That I'm a Christian: Basic Bible Studies for Youth

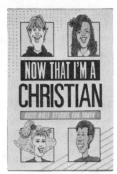

The plan is that if someone you know gets saved, you meet with him as soon as possible (if possible within 24 hours) and pray with him (see chapter 8). Then ask if you can meet with him once a week for the next eight weeks. Set up a regular time that is convenient for both of you. If possible, meet in one of your homes. If neither drive, make plans to get together before or after school or after a church meeting.

Give him Bible study number one before your first regular meeting. Encourage him to fill out the work sheet before the next week. At that meeting, review the work sheet, spend time discussing how he is doing in his spiritual walk, and give him work sheet number two. You follow the same process in the next meeting, reviewing work sheet two, and giving work sheet three for the next week, and so on.

At the last meeting you sign and present the certificate of completion. (There is space for your pastor or youth minister to sign it too.) At that time you can discuss what further plans need to be made. You will definitely want to work with your pastor or youth leader on this. Let them know who you are meeting with and give them a brief report when you are done with all eight studies. Discuss further activities.

Don't miss what is perhaps the most important part of the Bible studies—the fact that you are meeting with your friend on a regular basis. You aren't just doing homework assignments together. You are providing the personal support and encouragement that is so important to a growing Christian. So, you will obviously want to do more than just the work sheets.

Your *Now That I'm a Christian* packet will have complete instructions to help you follow through with a new Christian.

Conclusion

Our little baby never got a chance to live. But, the good news is that Cindy got another chance. During a Wednesday night discussion on the importance of caring for others, her name came up several times. Dana and three others became convinced that they had let Cindy down and needed to do something about it. So, they prayed and called. And they called and prayed. And after some reluctance on her part, Cindy was won back to the group and to the Lord. Their love and concern not only brought her back alive, but it helped her thrive as well. Today she's a senior at a Christian college and engaged to a Christian young man. She is sharing the same love she received from Jesus Christ and others.

To Think About, to Discuss, and to Do . . .

1. Read Rom. 12:3-8. Which of the spiritual gifts is most needed to help others survive and thrive as Christians?

2. Why is the amount of support provided by a church or youth group so important to whether or not a new Christian is easily able to embrace the faith?

3. Who has provided you with the time and energy to survive and thrive as a Christian?

4. Think of the teens and children from your church. Is there one person God would like you to begin praying for? Consider other ways you might become an encouragement to him.

5. Read through *Now That I'm a Christian: Basic Bible Studies for Youth,* or talk to your pastor or youth leader to discuss ways you can grow in your knowledge of what it means to be a Christian.

Mark Gilroy is senior curriculum editor in the youth department at the Church of the Nazarene Headquarters. He is a popular speaker and writer to youth and youth leaders.

Appendix

How to Use This Book in a Discipleship Group

Mark Gilroy

Reading this book will probably be a much more valuable experience if it is studied, discussed, and acted upon with others. A sharing-caring discipleship group will make the concepts easier to learn and the truth more powerful in your life. Note just a few of the dynamics a discipleship group will offer you.

Discipleship Groups . . .

- provide the satisfaction and bonding of working on a common task with a group of friends
- allow group members to verbalize fears, frustrations, and victories—and receive help when they realize that others share their same feelings
- provide a safe environment where persons can be affirmed and encouraged
- help us fine-tune our perspective, by critiquing us when we are way off base or need to consider another side of an issue
- help us be victorious by providing accountability—others are checking our progress
- are a tremendous place to meet with Jesus Christ—"For where two or three come together in my name, there am I with them" (Matt. 18:20).

Basic details of a discipleship group . . .

1. *Leader.* You need to find someone who will take responsibility to plan sessions and facilitate discussions. However, for the dynamics to be most effective, everyone should feel responsible for the success of the group. Everyone needs to share and participate. The leader's job is to encourage that to happen but not to feel the need to dominate discussion and format.

2. *Size.* An ideal size for a discipleship group is 12. (At least Jesus seemed to feel that way.) The group is still small enough to allow everyone a chance to share and participate. And it's not so big that individuals feel there is no time for them to make comments. If your group gets larger than 20, strongly consider finding additional leaders and breaking into subgroups.

3. *Time.* Perhaps you are making this a regularly scheduled Wednesday night youth group meeting and must work with a one-hour time limit. If you have flexibility, consider making each session 90 minutes. That way there is time for informal sharing, snacks, and other activities that will help each person relax. It will also provide more time to do role plays and other learning activities that will make the material more relevant. When your meeting is too rushed, it will discourage open sharing.

4. *Frequency of meeting.* Try to meet once a week. If your group is apart two weeks or more, it will be difficult to really bond and stay focused on the issue of evangelism. If your group can handle an intense setting, you might plan to work through this book during a retreat. You will probably have to limit how much material you cover so that other retreat dynamics can happen as well.

5. *Contract for accountability.* If this study is done during a regularly scheduled youth meeting, you will not be able to call for the accountability that you can with a volunteer meeting. If you do make this a distinct discipleship group study, consider a contract. It should include a commitment to attend sessions unless an emergency or illness arises. It should include the time and location(s) of your group meetings and the number of times your group will meet. If there is a set number of sessions, many will sign a contract, while they won't if it is open-ended. You might also include a clause that each person is expected to participate in discussions, activities, and homework assignments. That means that everyone is expected to have this book and read the chapter being discussed each week—prior to the group meeting.

6. *Participation.* Encourage everyone to get involved. However, when the sharing is more personal, no one should be pressured to say anything to the group that he doesn't want to say. Allow members to "pass" if necessary. If someone in your group consistently avoids participating, though, take the time to work with him individually. Perhaps he is struggling with an issue at home. Perhaps she doesn't feel accepted by others yet. Make this an opportunity for one-to-one ministry.

7. *Setting.* Ideally, your discipleship group should meet in a warm, informal setting, like somebody's family room. Chairs should be placed in a circle so that eye contact can be made with all members of the group. Rows encourage leader domination. That is not the purpose of a discipleship group. If you do meet in a home, be certain that there won't be distractions that make it impossible to share—a blaring TV in the next room, a boisterous puppy, etc.

8. *What to do.* Each session should include prayer, informal sharing, possibly a snack time, and of course, a study of evangelism. Each person should have a book and should be encouraged to have read the chapter being discussed before arriving. There are questions at the end of each chapter that will facilitate this time. Each person should have a Bible and a pen as well. Have supplies like paper and note cards on hand for writing assignments. There should be at-home assignments each week and a time the following week to report on them.

In addition to the discussion questions and activities at the end of each chapter, there is a brief activity "tip" for each session below that you can use to help as you design the 60- to 90-minute period.

9. *Keeping momentum.* The best way to keep momentum is to have stimulating sessions each week. Teens will return if they are being fed and challenged. The leader might also want to send weekly reminder cards and/or set up a phone chain where each group member has another person to remind of upcoming meetings from time to time. If your group bogs down, think of ways to change the setting—a week at a local park; determine if there's a problem that needs to be addressed—our group just hasn't got close to each other yet; evaluate your leadership—maybe more creativity needs to go into spicing up the teaching sessions.

10. *Starting and ending the group.* Your two most important sessions are your first and last. The first sets the tone. Make it fast-paced and positive. Be sure to let participants know what you hope and expect to happen in the next 8 to 12 weeks. Be sure to specifically note what the group will do for them and what they need to do for the group.

In the last session, help everyone know what was accomplished and not accomplished. Consider making it a real celebration of any victories that have taken place. You could have a dinner or pizza party. You might want to pass out serious and/or humorous awards—"person who was five minutes late the most," etc. Spend extra time having participants share what has happened to them during the time they were members of the discipleship group.

Announce future plans, but don't immediately move to form another discipleship group. Allow some breathing room. Announcing future plans and issues will allow members to consider them immediately, yet have time to reflect on what has happened in the last months. It also gives them something to look forward to if they particularly enjoyed this.

If you are the leader, you might also ask your stronger group members if they would consider leading a discipleship group on youth evangelism similar to what they just participated in.

Leader tips for each chapter

● To prepare a session on chapter 1, consider showing the Susie Shellenberger video *God's Vision for You* (VA-1995), a 35-minute presentation that also deals with the motivation for witnessing. You might invite someone from your church who has led others to Jesus Christ to give a 10-minute testimony on the same topic.

● To prepare a session on chapter 2, consider making number five at the end of the chapter an actual field trip. It is suggested that we conduct interviews, asking the question, "What is the greatest need in your life right now?" Equip your group members with clipboards, paper, and pens, and take them to a mall or other teen hangout to conduct the interviews. Gather together to discuss the results.

• To prepare a session on chapter 3, spend a good portion of your time on activity six at the end of the chapter. Individuals are to review the "Spiritual Decision Chart," and using Engel's main points, describe the process of how they became a Christian.

• To prepare a session on chapter 4, consider asking your group to be extremely open and honest with each other. Activity five at the end of the chapter asks the reader to have the courage to allow others to evaluate how well his life and relationships are actually a testimony to Jesus Christ. You might have one person at a time sit in the center of your circle, while others share openly and kindly what they feel that person's strengths and weaknesses are. If you have a group that is unkind to each other, you probably won't want to attempt this. Another way to do it would be for each person to put his name at the top of a sheet of paper and have everybody pass his sheet to the left. Each person would write comments on it, then pass the sheet to the left again, repeating the process until each person gets his own paper back. Allow time for group members to read their paper right then, and debrief the experience with the question: "What did you learn about yourself?"

• To prepare a session on chapter 5, create a number of role plays for your group members to perform. The idea is to help them practice opportunities for building conversational bridges that lead to spiritual matters. Some examples would include: a friend's father just died of cancer; your best friend's boyfriend has broken up with her; a friend begins talking about the changes that are occurring in Eastern Europe; your lab partner is talking about an upcoming Bon Jovi concert and wants to know if you're interested in going; a friend asks why your youth group meets on Wednesday nights.

• To prepare a session on chapter 6, make four different assignments, with two people working on each one, a week before your group meets. The assignment is for the twosome to carefully study one of the four methods of presenting the gospel, and be ready to teach it to the other group members. Encourage them to demonstrate the method, not just tell about it. Since chapter 6 is so long, this will help break up the material as well.

• To prepare a session on chapter 7, have your group serve as the church's "Youth Program Committee" for a simulation activity. They must prepare a report for the church board that looks backward and forward: (1) What our group did last year that reached out to unchurched teens. (2) What our group will do the next 12 months that will reach out to unchurched teens. Don't let their feedback remain vague. Encourage them to get specific and creative.

• To prepare a session on chapter 8, plan more role plays. Prepare note cards with six or seven situations where a person needs to receive spiritual counseling. More of the situations should focus on teens who need to become Christians.

• To prepare a session on chapter 9, discuss forming a "big brother"/"big sister" program for new Christians. There may be a number of new Christian teenagers already in your church who need someone to work through *Now That I'm a Christian: Basic Bible Studies for Youth* with them. Have your group members volunteer, and be sure to have the packet ready for them. You might want to prepare a commitment card, where your group members express willingness to be an encourager of new Christians. One other area of discussion might be teens who used to be part of your church but who have dropped out. Ask your group what responsibility they have for them and what, if anything, they can do about it.